Praise for *Against*

MW01103548

"The description of the US colonial war against Iraq in Ali Issa's *Against All Odds*, which includes testimonials from Iraqis on the ground, causes me to relive Israel's illegal, colonial, military occupation, and its oppressive and racist practices against my people. As a Palestinian woman who was born and grew up in a war zone, I have been struggling for freedom my entire life. The women of Iraq and Palestine have dedicated our lives to the same hopes and dreams. We all stand for social justice, liberation, and self-determination in our countries."

—Rasmea Odeh, Associate Director of the Arab American Action Network

"I am very grateful for Ali Issa's new book featuring stories of nonviolent resistance from the grassroots movements of Iraq. Too few have even noticed such a phenomenon emerging from this part of the world in the wake of decades of calamity inflicted on Iraq."

—Kathy Kelly, co-coordinator of Voices for Creative Nonviolence

"*Against All Odds* tells the story no mainstream media told about Iraq during the US occupation: that a widespread popular movement of Iraqis had been demanding the unconditional withdrawal of all occupation forces, calling for an end of sectarianism, demanding an end to security agreements with the occupiers, and becoming increasingly unified as time went on. Issa's book clearly shows how a home-grown grassroots truly Iraqi movement could well have, and still could, lead to Iraq being governed by Iraqis and the country finally becoming a true democracy."

—Dahr Jamail, author of *Beyond the Green Zone: Dispatches from an Unembedded Journalist in Occupied Iraq*

"Ali Issa's interviews with union organizers and other movement leaders in Iraq are especially valuable in providing first-hand accounts of a time and a place that has been difficult for many to think about in terms other than those of a 'failed state' and a 'shattered society.' The book is an important reminder that Iraqis rebuild, and they will rebuild again. They have no choice."

—Sara Pursley, Cotsen Postdoctoral Fellow, Society of Fellows, Princeton University

Against All Odds
Voices of Popular Struggle in Iraq

Ali Issa

Foreword by Vijay Prashad

TADWEEN PUBLISHING
Washington, DC

WAR RESISTERS LEAGUE
New York, NY

Printed in the United States of America
First Printing: May 2015
ISBN: 978-1-939067-16-6

This publication is co-published by and is produced in part with the support of War Resisters League. This publication also received support from the Middle East Program at George Mason University, with which the Arab Studies Institute is affiliated.

For Sabeeha Ali Issa (1941-2003)
and Buthaineh Ali Issa (1939-2014)

Table of Contents

Images:

Foreword

The Fires of Iraq
For Haifa Zangana

What remains of the dignity of Iraq? Such a bruised country: its society broken by the sanctions regime of the 1990s, its state shattered by the US occupation of the 2000s. In 2001, a United Nations (UN) report suggested that sixty percent of Iraqis had no regular access to clean water, while more than eighty percent of schools were in poor condition. Struck by a UN report that suggested that half a million children had died because of the sanctions regimes, the US ambassador to the United Nations Madeline Albright said that the US-driven sanctions policy nonetheless "was a price worth paying." UN Humanitarian Coordinator for Iraq Denis Halliday resigned from his post in 1998, saying that the program he had been tasked with overseeing was responsible for the death of over a million Iraqis. No society can withstand such pressure. When the United States eventually came in and swept away the remnants of the Iraqi state in 2003, the devastation was complete. Iraqi poet Sinan Antoon's lines, written in 2003, capture the full desolation in Iraq:

> My heart is a stork
> perched on a distant dome
> in Baghdad
> its nest made of bones
> its sky
> of death.[1]

That Iraq remains an entity is a testimony to the vitality of its history. But it barely remains. Terrible sectarianism pushed itself to the front of the clashes in the early years of the US occupation, as the US government relied on a sectarian structure to manage a broken society, and as Iraqi nationalist feints had to be smothered before an outright Iraqi revolt against the occupiers—mirrored on the revolt of the 1920s—could manifest.

Gunfire drowned out the stories of ordinary Iraqis, who built lives on a thread, or else fled inside or outside the country. Skirting the edge of battles, ordinary Iraqis lived out their lives—raising children, teaching them, working, making *maqluba* with less meat in it, and *shinina* with more water. Iraqi friends, uneasy about talking openly, are fearful of nothing in particular but everything in general. Old leftists, who had borne the brunt of the Saddam Hussein regime, look back fondly on those years because at least the politics was straightforward. New organizers who grew up in a collapsed society look forward to a world that is just a dream for which no hopeful signs currently exist.

This book privileges the voices of some Iraqi organizers and revolutionaries, whose realities and struggles stand outside of the Islamic State (IS) and the Asa'ib Ahl al-Haq, outside despondency and fear. On 25 February 2011, Iraqi men and women gathered at Baghdad's storied Tahrir Square, chanting *"illi ma ezoor al tahrir omra khasara"* [whoever is not at Tahrir Square is wasting their life]. The Iraqi government, backed by the United States, had already accused the protestors of being Ba'thists–terrorists–al-Qa'ida. But they were nothing of the sort. These were people from the Union of the Unemployed of Iraq and the Communist Party, the Organization of Women's Freedom in Iraq (OWFI), and the youth protest movement known as Where are My Rights?. OWFI's Yanar Mohammed noted, "You cannot force democracy through a gun." It is the people who have to rebuild their confidence in each other, build society, and then rebuild state institutions. Assassinations and disappearances took care of many of those who dared to take to the streets, including journalist and theatre director Hadi al-Mahdi. On his Facebook page, just hours before his murder, Mahdi wrote, "I am sick of seeing our mothers beg in the streets and I am sick of news of politicians' gluttony and of their looting of Iraq's riches."

The path of nonviolent civil disobedience was blocked in 2011, and then sent backward when Iraqi security forces massacred peaceful protestors in Hawija in April 2013. Documenting these incidents, Ali Issa's *Against All Odds* takes us from the 2011 Arab uprisings in Iraq, when organizers incubated hope for an alternative Iraqi future, to the emergence of IS in Falluja and Mosul, indeed much of Anbar and parts of Diyala provinces in 2013. Perhaps the natural child of the sanctions and the subsequent US occupation, the Islamic State has since done much to destroy any glimpse of those hopes. Other histories had been possible for Iraq, and indeed might yet be possible. The social basis for the Popular Movement to Save Iraq remains, even if in the shadows. It is the only force that could provide an alternative to the history of blood that stands before Iraq, the nest of bones, the sky of death.

Vijay Prashad
Hartford, Connecticut
November 2014

Preface

This book is the product of a process that spanned several years and would not have been possible without the generous support of friends, family, colleagues, and fellow travelers. Nearly all the pieces of this book are based on interviews I conducted in Arabic via e-mail, phone, or Skype, which I transcribed and translated into English. I entered into this work to fill a void that became more and more glaring the better I got to know Iraqi conditions on the ground. As with all organizing, building relationships has been central to putting this work together, and releasing it in this form is an expression of my gratitude.

I would first like to thank, for their generosity, vision, and courage, the following Iraqi movement leaders whom I interviewed: Hussam Abdullah, Falah Alwan, Nadia al-Baghdadi, Ali Eyal, Jannat Alghezzi, Ahmed Habib, Yanar Mohammed, Hashmeya Muhsin al-Saadawi, Akram Nadir, and Uday al-Zaidi. I would also like to thank those who put me in contact with Iraqi organizers on the ground: Asma al-Haidari and Hassan Jamal Jum'a, as well as Greg Muttitt, who provided in-depth knowledge and analysis first directly to Iraqi unions, which he then shared with me.

I would also like to thank the following friends and relatives who supported me through what was often a lonely and emotional process: Ali Adeeb, Sinan Antoon, Nadje Sadig Al-Ali, Nadia Awad, Ryvka Barnard, Andrew Bashi, Rosie Bsheer, Yasmeen Hanoosh, Kimber Heinz, Lindsay Hockaday, Hazem Jamjoum, Seelai Karzai, Amnah al-Mukhtar, Tej Nagaraja, Prachi Patankar, Brian Pickett, Laura Raymond, Zainab Saleh, Samah Selim, Joyce Wagner, Bryan Welton, Ora Wise, Tara Tabassi, Linda Thurston, Uruj Sheikh, and Shaheen Qureshi, among others.

To my parents Sabah Issa and Mary Issa, thank you for your years of support and love. To my aunts Sabeeha Issa and Buthaineh Issa, thank you for instilling in me a love of Arabic and so much more.

Last, there are two pieces that are not produced directly by me—"On the Kidnapping and Torture of Aya Al Lamie" by Yanar Mohammed and "On Recent Events in Mosul and Other Iraqi Cities" by Falah Alwan—which are republished here with permission. In addition, some of the reports and interviews originally published on *Jadaliyya* and the War Resisters League Blog have been modified for tone and clarity.

Introduction

Trauma not only destroys but creates.

> Nadje Al-Ali and Deborah Al-Najjar (eds.), *We Are Iraqis: Aesthetics and Politics in a Time of War*[2]

Terrorist or victim. Sunni or Shi'i or Kurd. Woman or oppressor-of-women. These words again and again frame stories of Iraqis, making them invisible, and erasing the experiences and possibilities they live out every day. The pages that follow reject that limited horizon, making space for Iraqis to tell their stories—and the stories of their struggles—in their own words.

A brief scan of the media reveals that even outlets which see themselves as working in solidarity with Iraqis focus almost exclusively on such rehearsed topics as the evils of the US government or former prime minister Nouri al-Maliki, the reach of regional players such as the Iranian regime, and the Islamic State (IS). "Iraq is splitting into three parts," writes Patrick Cockburn in a 6 April 2006 article[3] for the *London Review of Books* entitled (in the print version) "Diary: The End of Iraq." Several years later, in 2013, Cockburn forecasts the end of Sykes-Picot—that secret agreement which allegedly delineated the borders between Iraq and Syria, as well as in the rest of the Middle East—as another "end to Iraq."[4] Predicting an end for Iraqis, beset by geopolitics and domestic opportunism, is not just common but systematic. Its effect is that people actually living in Iraq—their communities, dreams, and victories, big and small—are again and again made invisible. Getting to the "real players," which is a term that always refers to those who can supply the biggest guns, is how journalists, activists, and academics are taken seriously when writing about Iraq. How can we understand politics, economics, culture, or society anywhere without the main protagonists, people? More specifically, what happens when we seek out Iraqi progressives who have been *actively* struggling to fight oppressive forces that are mutually constitutive and reinforcing?

History is often another missing element in Iraq's story. That story does not begin with Obama announcing airstrikes on IS in September 2014, nor does it begin in 2003 with the US invasion and occupation. Memories of the US role in supporting dictatorship and condoning torture and extermination in Iraq stretch back decades and are very much present in Iraqis' minds and consciousness, even if many around the world have forgotten or have chosen to forget this troubling past. Iraqis themselves often trace their stories back to when the United States and several European governments backed Saddam Hussein's authoritarianism—which included the perpetration of the Halabja massacre in the north of Iraq and catastrophic military adventures in the 1980s—and then imposed some of the most comprehensive sanctions on a state following the 1990 Gulf War. For many Iraqis, the 2003 US-led war and eight-year occupation is a culmination of the previous tragedies that have beset the country and its people. The US occupation brought in a new class of autocrats, death squads—sometimes directly supported by Iran—and a new sectarian order, enshrined by decision-makers in Washington. These policies were actually carried out by handpicked Iraqi exiles who came back to Iraq on the backs of US tanks, which opened up the space for massive Iranian influence. Indeed, the Iranian government has been the clearest beneficiary of the weakening of the Iraqi state, with various militias that are wreaking havoc in Iraq today having direct Iranian ties.

As Jannat Alghezzi of the Organization of Women's Freedom in Iraq (OWFI) recently told me:

> If there were a US politician sitting in front of me, I would say to them that, in 2003 and immediately after, Paul Bremer [the top civilian administrator of the former Coalition Provisional Authority in Iraq] and his government really championed political Islamists, giving them real power. This is the same political Islam that has brought us to where Iraq is today.

Adding to the overall violence of occupation, the new Iraqi leaders subjected all organized, independent opposition to harassment, torture, or death. The latest development in this history is the rise of IS, the violent, sectarian, and reactionary force that, as of this writing, continues to commit almost weekly massacres and mass rapes while often enslaving captured communities, which the movement vows it will ethnically cleanse.

As many have noted, knowledge of IS—its precise sources of support, regional and local alliances, and recruitment strategies—is difficult to tease out in a rapidly evolving situation. Nevertheless, it is clear that their ability to seize large swaths of northern and western Iraq—including Iraq's second largest city, Mosul, as well as sizable parts of eastern Syria—was made possible by, and is directly tied to, the legacy of the US occupation of Iraq.

The sectarian and authoritarian system that the occupation established and institutionalized was, and is, sustained by local forces of reaction and repression:

from cynical Iraqi politicians to Syria's Bashar al-Asad, who is known to have released fundamentalist forces from Syrian jails to justify the ongoing and murderous repression that he used to silence the 2011 Syrian uprising.[5]

With this in mind, the question arises: What is the value of progressive Iraqi voices now? Hearing Iraqis speak about their political work, analyses, struggles, and visions allows people all over the world—academics, journalists, organizers, or artists—to zoom in from the broader geopolitics and elite-centered interests and build a commitment to understanding what Iraqis are doing on the ground. It is my hope that engaging with these nuances and complexities can be a radically humbling act that curbs a constant centering of US and "big player" policies to the exclusion of Iraqis working and struggling locally. People in Iraq are trying out political solutions and strategies in practice, and media commentators and solidarity organizers around the world would do well to take those living efforts as their starting points. I also hope that these words and images will bring attention to larger questions of accountability and justice: how to begin to think and act in solidarity with the courageous fight Iraqis are waging against multiple nightmarish forces.

My role in this story begins with my father, Sabah Ali Issa, who was born in Baghdad in 1944. I was born in Texas in 1980 and visited Iraq only once in 1986. Beginning in the early 1990s, I spent the summers in Amman, Jordan, where my relatives had moved to avoid the harshness of the sanctions, a familiar story in the Iraqi diaspora. While writing my thesis on Iraqi literature and the social movements of the 1960s years later in graduate school, I was also becoming increasingly politicized through anarchist cooperative bookstores and friends who worked with construction workers to build a worker center and rights movement across Texas. I often yearned to connect my pride in Iraq's history to the actually existing potential of Iraq's present. Flash forward to New York City, 2009, when interpreting for an Iraqi labor union delegation gave me that chance. It was then that I had the honor and privilege of getting to know political organizers working on the ground in Iraq, who had much to teach me and were beyond generous in answering my incessant questions. Around that time I began documenting their work, first on a very basic Wordpress blog called *Iraq Left: On Iraqi Organizing and Movement Building Now*, then alternatively on the blog of War Resisters League—where I currently work as a national field organizer—and the groundbreaking *Jadaliyya*, an e-zine on Arab politics and culture.[6]

The range of perspectives below—though striving for breadth and diversity —can make no claim to comprehensiveness, even among the "progressive" (roughly defined) views within Iraq's borders. The brief interview with Iraqi Kurdistan labor organizer Akram Nadir notwithstanding, time constraints—but, above all, electricity blackouts that interrupted many of my Skype interviews and the violence that has caused mass migrations—prevented me from including a broader cross section of progressive Kurdish organizers, as well as voices from Iraq's embattled western and northern regions. I hope to make up that gap in the near future.[7]

Against All Odds begins with a series of reports from 2011, along with statements from various participants in Iraq's uprising. The importance of that time and spirit becomes clear with how many interviewees refer back to it as a watershed. In the words of Ismaeel Dawood of the Iraqi Civil Society Solidarity Initiative: "[In those] 'Days of Rage,' Iraq was covered—overtaken—by sit-ins and protests from the north to the south, demanding social justice . . . ." I explore what "social justice" meant to different strands of the groups participating in the 2011 protests, what the protestors were asking for, and how they did so, in addition to the repression meted out against them and the subsequent media silence that attempted to keep them invisible. Following reports on these protests, statements from Iraqis to both Occupy Wall Street and the Syrian uprising highlight the key role that cross-regional and global solidarity plays in the vision of some Iraqi organizers.

In section II, "Interviews," I go further in-depth by interviewing several leaders from across Iraq's movements, beginning with Uday al-Zaidi; brother of "the shoe thrower" and prominent figure in Iraq's 2011 protests. After that, a prominent electricity sector unionist in Basra shares the story of the Federation of Oil Unions' struggle—and partial victory—over the US government's privatizing "oil law" in 2007. Next, the president of the Federation of Workers' Councils and Unions in Iraq analyzes the Anbar protests in early 2013, an analysis that turned out to predict much of the events that would impact all of Iraqi society throughout 2014—namely, the repression of the opposition movements and the gains of IS.

Next is an interview with the founder of shakomako.net, a website that aims to serve as an empowering virtual community and media source for Iraqis around the world. Thereafter, an interview with an organizer from the Save the Tigris and Iraqi Marshes Campaign sheds light on Iraq's environmental crises and activists. The next interview explores OWFI, one of the very few organizations directly opposing US intervention while actively working with refugees running from the horrors of IS violence.

Finally, this section ends with an interview with a visionary labor organizer working in Iraqi Kurdistan, analyzing economic conditions in the north, as well as the regional Iraqi Kurdish government's cynical use of the spread of IS to silence and marginalize its opposition.

The founder of the Solidarity and Brotherhood Yazidi Organization, Hussam Abdullah, himself a refugee who also escaped IS attacks, told me in an interview that the present IS campaign to destroy so much of Iraq's historical diversity and ethnically cleanse Yazidis from Iraq is "trying to crush hope." This crisis of hope is further elaborated in what the Baghdad-based artist Ali Eyal—who was affiliated with Sada,[8] a project that supported emerging visual artists in Iraq— recently told me:

> You could also ask what is art's take on the destruction that is happening? What is its perspective? What does art say about what Iraq is going through? What will it look like? What will be its form? . . . If only you knew how much hope Iraqis have. For example, yesterday Kadhimiya [a neighborhood in Baghdad] was bombed. The next day we were out there making art. [In Iraq] we are strange. On the same street where there is an attack, people are walking the next day as if nothing happened . . . Iraqis remain ordinary Iraqis like you and me. Their sole preoccupation is to survive, to persevere.

The nature of Iraq's perseverance and how it relates to the visions described in *Against All Odds* is something worthy of far more attention. It holds stories of remarkable cruelty, courage, and tenacity. It also holds out the possibility of popular struggle leading to a just Iraq to come.

SECTION I
Iraq Reports

On 25 February 2011, inspired by the uprisings across the Arab world, the "Iraqi Day of Rage," a weekly Friday protest cycle, began in many of Iraq's major cities. It was the rejuvenation of a protest movement that the Iraqi government had brutally suppressed since 2003. The demands, explored in detail below, were diverse, ranging from addressing chronically high unemployment and the lack of services like electricity to opposing the entire US-installed sectarian regime and occupation. Certain Fridays were themed around particular issues, with 18 March, for example, dubbed "Friday of the Imprisoned," drawing attention to thousands of Iraqi political prisoners and demanding their release.

Leaders, like the Zaidi brothers (Uday, Thurgham, and Muntazar, the latter famed for throwing a shoe at George W. Bush in December 2008) began to emerge, and other civil society leaders affiliated with labor and women's groups got heavily involved. Several popular Iraqi Facebook protest pages appeared, and by 25 April, gatherings and open-ended sit-ins sometimes reached the tens of thousands. In the northern city of Mosul, protestors called for a general strike, which froze all commerce and even pushed the local governor Atheel al-Nujaifi to back the protests and support the defiance of a government-imposed curfew.

The explicitly national character of this movement—including in Iraq's Kurdish cities of Erbil and Sulaymaniyah—which was set against a system of identity politics that continues to dominate discourses on Iraq, is worthy of note. Describing the protest movement of 2011, Uday al-Zaidi of the Popular Movement to Save Iraq identified the concrete shifts that the protests had forced by June while insisting on Iraq's sectarian system as the true target.

The sectarian quota system to which Zaidi refers is an unofficial "power-sharing" agreement that divides power in almost all of Iraq's political institutions among "representatives" of various ethnicities, sects, and religions. The Coalition Provisional Authority under Paul Bremer initiated this system in 2003. This system has also been strongly supported regionally by the governments of Iran, Turkey, and Jordan, to name a few. The fact that this system is neither enshrined in any law, nor an amendment to Iraq's constitution—and is intimately connected to a particular kind of identity politics brought by Iraqi elites in exile —is essential to its functioning. What the following documentation of the protests makes plain is that these conventions are far from "age-old" and are vulnerable to challenge. These realities will shape the course of any fight against them, as well as the waves of ferocity bent on defending or replacing them with a vision of Iraq ever more divided.

1 | Defying Iraq's Police State
22 March 2011

According to various Iraqi Facebook pages, 18 March 2011 was dubbed "Friday of the Imprisoned," which led to several thousand protesters marching in Baghdad, Ramadi, Falluja, and other cities amid extreme state security measures, checkpoints—centered especially around Baghdad's Green Zone—and the use of sound bombs, tear gas, and sometimes live ammunition to break up the demonstrations.[9] The call for a focus on prisons came partially in response to a prison revolt that took place in Tikrit on 13 March.[10] However, many of the protest organizers from the past several Fridays (the day demonstrations have been held regularly since 18 February) have been arrested, highlighting the fact that Iraq has had a soaring prison population since 2007.[11] Protesters chanted "Free government prisoners," "Improve social services," "Bring down Maliki's government," and "Leave, leave occupier," during marches.

2| Occupying the Bases
29 March 2011

On 22 March 2011, five Iraqi grassroots organizations announced an initiative to target "the occupier and its agents": US military bases and Iraq's Maliki-led government. Riding the recent wave of sizable Iraqi demonstrations against government corruption, lack of social services, Iraq's prison industrial complex, and a broken sectarian political system, the sit-ins planned for 9 April 2011 are the first to call out the US occupation as a central, persistent cause of the shattered social reality that millions of Iraqis face every day.[12] A new zeal and organizational drive inspired by the recent Arab uprisings has allowed the grievances laid out during the past month of weekly protests to coalesce. Two communiqués, co-signed by the Popular Movement to Save Iraq, the Popular Front to Save Kirkuk, the Student and Youth Organization of a Free Iraq, the Movement in Steadfast Basra to Liberate the South, and the Iraqi Association of the Tribes of Southern and Central Iraq, outline their demands and the means by which they hope to achieve them.[13] These demands include

- the unconditional departure of the occupying forces;

- the revocation of the security agreement which violates the sovereignty and independence of Iraq;

- the revocation of the sectarian and ethnic quota system in the political process;

- the building of a civil state through transparent elections, without the interference of the occupation forces or any foreign forces, especially Iran;

- the release of innocent prisoners from occupation and government prisons;

- the disclosure of the location of secret prisons that are scattered all over Iraq's provinces;

- carrying out the demands of our people which were outlined during the "Uprising of Rage" on 25 February;

- the formation of an independent judicial committee to investigate the actions of the security forces against peaceful demonstrators [involved in protests over this last month].

The communiqué continues:

> The launch of a long-term sit-in in all Iraqi provinces to mark
> the eighth anniversary of the brutal US occupation of our
> precious Iraq on Saturday, 9 April 2011 [. . .] This sit-in will not
> last hours or days, but will continue night and day until the
> protesters' demands are met [. . .] For our sit-ins we will set up
> tents in front of US military bases, which are located in every
> Iraqi province. We ask all patriotic individuals and forces that
> oppose the occupation to participate in this demonstration.[14]

The United States maintains fourteen massive military installations in Iraq
along with dozens of smaller ones. With the Bush administration having pushed
for fifty-eight permanent bases[15] during the drafting of the US-Iraq status of
forces agreement, their fate under the Obama administration and the planned
post-2011 "withdrawal" remains unclear.[16]

Among those leading the call to "occupy the bases" is Uday al-Zaidi. As
vocal organizers of the last month of protests, both Uday and his brother
Muntazar have been harassed, assaulted, and detained by the Iraqi authorities.[17]

Large media outlet coverage of this mobilization call has been scant but
included brief stories on Al Jazeera Arabic[18] and local Iraqi media. The Iraqi
blogosphere, though, has been abuzz with talk of the planned protests and, more
broadly, about how to channel the protest momentum and mobilize for lasting
change in Iraq.

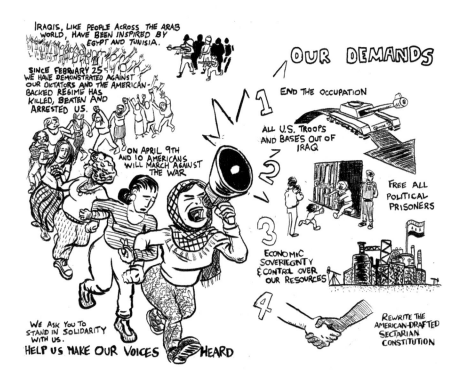

IRAQIS, LIKE PEOPLE ACROSS THE ARAB WORLD, HAVE BEEN INSPIRED BY EGYPT AND TUNISIA.

SINCE FEBRUARY 25, WE HAVE DEMONSTRATED AGAINST OUR DICTATORS AND THE AMERICAN-BACKED REGIME HAS KILLED, BEATEN AND ARRESTED US.

ON APRIL 9TH AND 10 AMERICANS WILL MARCH AGAINST THE WAR

WE ASK YOU TO STAND IN SOLIDARITY WITH US.

HELP US MAKE OUR VOICES HEARD

OUR DEMANDS

1 END THE OCCUPATION

2 ALL U.S. TROOPS AND BASES OUT OF IRAQ

FREE ALL POLITICAL PRISONERS

3 ECONOMIC SOVERIEGNTY & CONTROL OVER OUR RESOURCES

4 REWRITE THE AMERICAN-DRAFTED SECTARIAN CONSTITUTION

13

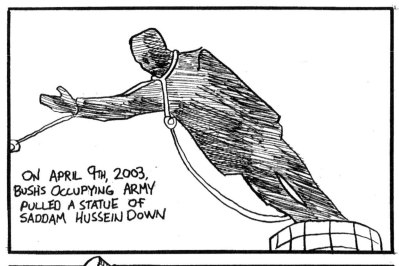

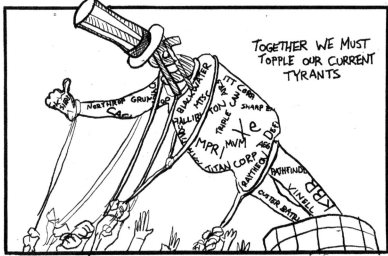

"April 9th Iraq Protest" (2011) by Ethan Heitner

3 | Protests Continue
22 April 2011

The city of Mosul in northern Iraq has become the epicenter of the continuing protests this week.

An estimated three hundred Iraqis initially set up tents in the northern Iraqi city of Mosul to demand an end to the US occupation, the release of political prisoners, the rewriting of the constitution, and the departure of what they call the Green Zone government, headed by Nouri al-Maliki.

Among the dozens of grassroots organizations calling for sit-ins in front of US military bases, two of the most prominent taking part in Mosul are the Popular Movement to Save Iraq and the Free Iraqis of Mosul. Contingents of Iraqis from as far south as Nasiriyah and Basra are at the Mosul sit-in being held in what has become known as Prisoner's Square. The calls for nationwide demonstrations in Iraq comes in the wake of high-ranking US politicians, including Senator John Kerry, Vice President Joe Biden, and most recently Secretary of State Robert Gates, implying that US forces may stay past the December 2011 deadline.

Last week, Iraqi Facebook pages, administered directly by protest organizers, reported that government security forces encircled their camp, surveilled and taunted them, and called on them to end their sit-in.[19] Protesters also reported that a low-flying US military helicopter swept toward the demonstrators in what was interpreted as an attempt to intimidate them. Their response, captured in the 13 April 2011 clip "Iraqi Protestors Throw Shoes at American Helicopters," was to throw dozens of shoes toward the helicopter, while asking for an investigation into the military vehicle's purpose.[20]

Dozens of women have joined the demonstrations, calling for the end of the US occupation and the release of their sons and brothers, who are being held in both Iraqi and US-run prisons throughout Iraq. This week, tribal leaders from nearby Anbar Province joined the Mosul protests as well.

As of today, reports estimate the growing crowds in Mosul to number in the thousands, comprised of many young people who were last seen marching toward the fourth bridge, where they were stopped by government troops and prevented from joining other protesters in the square.

Demonstrators are insistent on continuing their sit-in until all their demands are met, foremost of which are as follows: (1) the complete departure of the US occupying forces, (2) no extension of the security agreement between the Maliki government and the United States, and (3) the release of innocent prisoners.

4| Mosul Sit-in Grows Amid Violent Crackdowns
19 May 2011

By 25 April, the sit-in in Mosul calling for the withdrawal of US troops, the release of prisoners, and a change in Maliki's government was approaching a mass scale. Some estimates put the crowds in the tens of thousands. Artists of all types were joining in to create visuals with a message and perform political poetry.[21] One poet began with a verse about George W. Bush and was greeted with loud cheers from the crowd:

> He came to Baghdad
> and wanted the people to call him "pasha"
> the first call came
> two shoes fired at him like bullets from a machine gun . . . .

Chants directed at Prime Minister Nouri al-Maliki were for the first time interspersed with those ominous four words of the Arab uprising: "*Al-sha'b yurid isqat al-nizam.*" [The people want the downfall of the regime].[22]

During the last week of April, Iraqi authorities attempted to impose a curfew in Mosul and then violently cracked down on those defying it. Interestingly, Atheel al-Nujaifi—the governor of Nineveh Province, where Mosul is located—denounced Maliki's violent crackdown. Al Jazeera Arabic also reported on how Nujaifi and protest organizers called for a general strike in Mosul on Tuesday, 25 April in reaction to the attacks on protesters.[23]

Protest movement spreads to other cities

Finally, on the eighteenth day of sit-ins (26 April), Mosul security forces loyal to Maliki were able to disperse the demonstrators and prevent others from entering the city. While this was a blow to Iraq's protest movement, there had already been calls for similar sit-ins in Kut, Basra, and Ramadi.

The Ramadi sit-in is ongoing and has reached sizable proportions. It is centered on another square, which has been renamed Tahrir (Liberation) Square.

In the meantime, large Friday protests have continued in Baghdad's Tahrir Square, including on 5 May.

While not yet directly involved in the Iraqi protest movement, oil workers in the city of Basra have shown they are also part of the recent wave of defiance. On

Monday, 9 May, hundreds of employees of the South Iraq Oil Company went on strike, protesting against corruption and low wages.[24]

Iraqi delegation travels to Spain

In an attempt to raise international awareness, members of the Popular Movement to Save Iraq, including prominent organizer Uday al-Zaidi, visited various cities in Spain as part of a delegation hosted by Campaña Estatal contra la Ocupación y por la Soberanía de Iraq (National Campaign Against the Occupation and for Iraqi Sovereignty, CEOSI).[25]

Maliki's "100 Days" and massive protests planned for 7 June

Once protests began in earnest in Iraq on 25 February, Prime Minister Nouri al-Maliki announced that his cabinet had one hundred days to address "corruption." The end of the hundred days is 7 June, and Iraqi organizers, never having much faith in Maliki's promises to begin with, are gearing up for mass action to point out how inept and ineffective their present government is.

This issue becomes all the more relevant in the wake of the recent parade of US officials to Iraq—the latest being House Speaker John Boehner—who have announced the possibility of the United States staying on past the 31 December 2011 deadline for withdrawal. Maliki himself stated publicly as recently as last week that if seventy percent of the Iraqi parliament agrees to it, he will consider keeping US forces in Iraq beyond the deadline. This has inflamed the sensibilities of the Iraqi protest movement whose chief demand is the complete removal of US forces.

5| Maliki Runs Out of Days
6 June 2011

Iraqi grassroots organizers have marked 7 June as the "Day of Retribution," with nationwide protests and sit-ins being planned against the US occupation as well as Maliki's regime. The timing coincided with Maliki's own deadline, set exactly one hundred days ago, to address the protest movement's demands. "Changes will be made in light of the evaluation of results," Maliki said in a statement in late February, referring to his cabinet members and their performance.[26]

In response, a recently released call to action by the Popular Movement to Save Iraq grassroots organization expresses a broadly held sentiment among Iraqis: the government's promises are not to be trusted. In a statement, the Popular Movement to Save Iraq declared: "We admit that we were not really waiting." Seeing the date as a marker to draw more dissatisfied Iraqis into the protest movement, the statement continues: "But the end of the hundred-day period, [with the government] having achieved nothing whatsoever, was the fuse we were waiting for."

The actions and demonstrations mentioned above have varied in their size, intensity, and intent. Over the past hundred days, Friday demonstrations in Baghdad's Tahrir Square have persistently numbered in the thousands. The grievances of those protesters included that a lack of services, such as reliable electricity, has persisted after nearly a decade of a new regime. Crucially though, demands have also often included the immediate withdrawal of US occupation forces, the release of political prisoners, and the revocation of the informal sectarian quota system. Such important facts are often omitted by what little coverage Iraq receives. A 29 May story by the news agency *Aswat al-Iraq*, for example, only mentions protesters "demanding an end [to] corruption, the improvement of public services and living standards of the people, as well as putting an end to unemployment in the country."

These broader-aimed protests were most prominent during a twenty-day-long sit-in in the northern city of Mosul, launched on 9 April, eight years to the day after Baghdad fell to the occupation forces. Iraqi blogs and Facebook pages are attempting to marshal the energy of that sustained action for 7 June, recalling that it grew to the tens of thousands, contained a lively, celebratory air, included political poetry and theater performances, and even pushed the governor of Mosul, Atheel al-Nujaifi, to openly defy Maliki's forces and defend the right of

Iraqis to demonstrate. In response to Maliki's threats of a clampdown—backed by live ammunition—nearly the entire city went on a general strike on 25 May.[27]

Another significant development in the Iraqi protest movement is the coordination between groups, as well as the clarity of their demands. Mainly through Facebook, a consistent source of photos, videos, and statements has become the media office of the Great Iraqi Revolution and the February 25 Revolution Coalition.

Finally, in a joint statement signed by several groups—such as the Movement to Liberate the South [of Iraq], the Organization of Students of a Free Iraq, the National Organization of Tribal Leaders of the South and the Central Euphrates, the Movement of Rising Iraqis, the Coalition to Support the Iraqi Revolution, and the Movement of Iraqi Youth—a positive alternative to Iraq's present reality begins to emerge.

Whose "Regime"?

Observers of the Iraqi protest movement cannot help but notice that its numbers swell whenever there is a visit by a US diplomat to the Green Zone. The 25 February "Day of Rage" came immediately after hints from the State Department were made public that US forces may need to remain. Likewise, many slogans in all of Iraq's public squares were responses to statements Joe Biden, John Kerry, or Robert Gates had recently made. A key development in this regard was Maliki's shift from denying the possibility of a US troop presence past the 2011 year-end deadline—agreed upon in the 2008 status of forces agreement —to saying on 10 May, "You want to make me say yes or no before I gather the national consensus? I will not say it."

The demands for political freedoms, transparency, an end to corruption, and due process rather than the arbitrary force exercised by police are similar to the demands of other pro-democracy movements in the Arab world. This has come alongside a call for self-determination against an over eight-year US occupation and a clear Iranian influence on the Maliki-led coalition government, making Iraq unique. It also makes Maliki's regime especially glaring in its lack of legitimacy.

As Uday al-Zaidi, the lead organizer of the Popular Movement to Save Iraq put it: "Our central demand is and will continue to be an end to the occupation, and an end to this political process which is built on a sectarian quota system." Perhaps sensing how vulnerable the top of the pyramid is, Iraqi police—and sometimes the military—have launched a severe crackdown in the run-up to 7

June, arresting, questioning, and sometimes torturing activists and their supporters. The crackdown has been so blatantly repressive that even international human rights organizations like Amnesty International, which have often been very quiet about Iraq, have condemned these actions and called for the release of those detained—notably, prominent blogger Ahmed Alaa al-Baghdadi.[28]

The tactics—which include transmitting rally locations and times by writing them on paper currency—seem to be outrunning the repression for the moment. This was also known to be an effective method of communication in Egypt, where, like in Iraq, the vast majority of people are without access to Facebook.

In the words of Uday al-Zaidi, "This has shown us once and for all that terrorism and the Iraqi government are two sides of the same coin."

[This report was originally published on The Indypendent *website*[29]*]*

6| Thurgham al-Zaidi Freed and Vows to Continue Protest
3 July 2011

On Monday, 26 June, protest organizer and leader of the Popular Movement to Save Iraq Thurgham al-Zaidi was kidnapped by an unknown group wearing civilian clothes. Read an English translation of the Popular Movement's communiqué below as well as Uday al-Zaidi's Facebook update for further details.[30]

Communiqué 46

> In the name of God, the most Gracious, the most Merciful
>
> Re: The Kidnapping of the activist Thurgham al-Zaidi
>
> The Popular Movement to Save Iraq and organizations in the coalition condemn the kidnapping of the protest organizer Thurgham al-Zaidi by thugs from the Green Zone. Thurgham al-Zaidi was kidnapped by a group wearing civilian clothes near the Iraqi army checkpoint of Division 11 on Monday, 26 June 2011. The army did not respond to this kidnapping at all, indicating it had been planned beforehand. The security forces had detained him in the past without ever releasing original arrest papers, showing again the utter powerlessness of the Iraqi courts over the executive branch, which arrests whoever it wants, whenever it wants, with absolutely no judicial process! When we call for the government to stop randomly arresting people who have committed no crimes, we hold the government responsible for the life of Mr. Thurgham al-Zaidi. We demand his immediate release in addition to the release of all the innocent prisoners in occupation and government jails. We also ask legal and human rights organizations inside and outside of Iraq to intervene and push for Zaidi's release as well as the release of all prisoners in occupied Iraq who suffer from psychological and physical torture. These arrests violate international human rights norms which the Green Zone government continues to trample on.

The Popular Movement to Save Iraq

Co-signer Organizations: Movement to Free the South, Covenant on the Rights of Detained, Popular Front to Save Kirkuk, the Iraqi Organization of Tribes of the South and Central Euphrates, Students and Youth of a Free Iraq, and Rising Iraqis

Occupied Baghdad
 30 June 2011

Update:

> Thank God and everyone who stood by him, your brother Thurgham has been released. He was subjected to severe torture for his participation in protests. This is the tax that the youth of Iraq are paying for freedom and for booting out our two occupations, the US and Iranian. Maliki does not scare us. Thurgham has assured me that he is coming out to the protest this Friday along with his little son Haydar to say to Maliki, "If you kill the big ones, the little ones are coming after you!"

Uday al-Zaidi, personal Facebook page
3 July 2011

7 | Exoneration, Electricity, and the Movement on Television
22 July 2011

"Friday after Friday, until we kick Maliki out!" was a popular chant in Iraq two weeks ago and has remained in use until today for what groups have called the "Friday of Iraqi Exoneration." Despite reports of extreme, almost absurd, security restrictions in parts of Iraq—such as in Baghdad's Tahrir Square, where protesters were not allowed to bring water bottles, posters, or even pens and markers, which they had planned to use to create posters on the spot—there was enough of a turnout in Baghdad for Maliki's security forces to break them up by firing live rounds in the air. There were also reports of sizable rallies in Ramadi and across Anbar.

Many Iraqi organizers though, such as Asma al-Haidari and Yanar Mohammed, have noted that over the last month, the number of protesters has fluctuated dramatically from week to week. Aside from the now expected severe repression, there is also the very real issue of scorching summertime temperatures, which have reached highs of 50 to 60 degrees Celsius [122 to 140 Fahrenheit]. This is coupled with the fact that for the past several months, there have been serious lobbying efforts by many Iraqi sectors to address chronic electricity shortages before the summer heat began. This was addressed directly by a recent statement from the media office of the Great Iraqi Revolution when they wrote:

> Those who negotiated with the government in the past are now coming back to the square, after they were used by the government who wooed them with false promises. Let those who negotiated say, "the government deceived us!" [. . .] This government that could not meet the demands of a handful of individuals will be unable to meet the demands of the people in general, whether those demands concern services or the legitimate desire that the occupation leave . . .[31]

Indeed, rather than meeting Iraqi demands for power to run air conditioners and fans, the Iraqi Ministry of Electricity seems focused on closing a "mega deal" with the Australian energy giant Alstom Grid through the Turkish company Calik Energy and planning an energy and electricity conference in Istanbul for late September.[32]

Finally, there is word that the privately-owned and sometimes pro-protest Iraqi television station Al Sharqiya is in the process of shooting a drama series in Cairo, featuring the Iraqi youth movement and the struggles of its now five months of protest. The series will premiere during this coming Ramadan.[33]

8 | "Any Nation That Stands Against Its Oppressor": Iraq-Syria Solidarity
16 September 2011

As the Syrian uprising enters its sixth month and shows no sign of turning back, the Syrian people took note of the Iraqi government's strong support for Syrian president Bashar al-Asad's regime, who has been brutally repressing Syrians with full military force. In mid-August, Iraqi prime minister Nouri al-Maliki was reported to have met with Syrian business luminaries to create "stronger economic ties."[34] In response, the coalition of Syrian committees wrote a statement to the Iraqi people, one that in turn received a response from the Great Iraqi Revolution, which is translated below.[35]

> Open Letter to the Heroic Syrian Revolution
>
> 22 August 2011
>
> We, along with all Iraqis, have read the message you addressed to Iraq and its people, urging them to take a position on the Syrian revolution. Accordingly, we give you our answer as we look forward to your freedom that you are fueling with the blood of free men, freedom you express through chants recited by Syrians young and old, singing for all the free men and women around the world: "God . . . Syria . . . and Freedom only."
>
> Know, oh, brothers that we are living [in] an era of "new blood," after living half a century under tyranny and injustice. God has honored all of us with a change brought by a new generation that our "leaders" mistakenly thought could not offer anything, thinking their regimes were successful in taming and alienating them from the true meaning of resistance against their unjust monarchs. But the will of God has made these young men, among them Syrian young men, into swords at the throats of the tyrants, battling them with bare chests and angry voices calling for freedom. They use modern-day technology that today's dictators kept from us for decades as a method of communication, replacing the old way of underground meetings that activists used in the past.
>
> We approve of your blessed revolution, support its youth, and bless its steps as we anticipate its success and the accomplishment of its

goals. This is our stance on every revolution that is led by any nation that stands against its oppressor; and as far as we know this is the stance of all Iraqis on your revolution, as well as the stance of all people of conscience.

As for the Iraqi government that stands in support of the regime of murder and blood, its position is predictable because the tyrants overlap in a shared project sponsored by a regional power whose goals are no longer hidden to anyone. And do not forget that the politicians of the new Iraq were also embraced in the past by the same regime that is killing and targeting you.

Finally, we wish to bring our Syrian revolutionary brothers' attention to the importance of preserving the peacefulness of their revolution and its noble objectives, not to give those who are slaves to occupiers a chance to coopt your agenda. Maintain the revolution's national agenda so it may shine with its honorable goals, so that your grandchildren grow full of pride knowing that you created this revolution with your own two hands.

Know that your triumph is inevitable, no matter how long it takes. For you are more worthy of Syria than a regime that has unleashed its army and allowed it to kill its own people while not once aiming a bullet at the occupied Golan Heights over these past decades.

Be assured that your coming victory will strengthen us to resist our tyrants and the occupiers that sponsor them.

Till we meet soon, God willing, under the shade of new regimes that draw their legitimacy from the will of the people and are not taken in by the unjust among them, who belittle their potential.

May God bless your martyrs' souls, and may they dwell in heaven.

May God heal your wounded.

Go under God's protective watch.

The Youth of the Great Iraqi Revolution

9 | On the Kidnapping and Torture of Aya Al Lamie
30 September 2011

The following statement was issued in English by the president of the Organization of Women's Freedom in Iraq (OWFI).[36]

> Although the number of demonstrators has decreased in Iraq's Tahrir Square, Aya Al Lamie insisted on joining the demonstrators every Friday of the last few months. She insisted on putting a woman's face on the Tahrir demonstrations and cooperated with all the organized groups in the square.
>
> In the afternoon of Friday, 30 September 2011, toward the end of the demonstration, a group of security men dressed in civilian clothing surrounded her, carried and threw her into the trunk of a car which they parked next to the square, in what looked like sectarian mob kidnappings that took place under the eyes of the police and the army. This has become common practice in the last few months in Tahrir.
>
> Twenty-year-old Aya was taken to a security facility in al-Jadiriyah, Baghdad where she was beaten by thugs using sticks and whipping her back and arms with cables. She was released at 5:00 p.m. after being told: "This was a first warning!"
>
> The thugs of Maliki have proven again that they are the enemies of women. They persist in establishing a despotic rule in Iraq with the blessings of the forces of occupation. If not for the occupation, the people of Iraq would have ousted Saddam Hussein through the struggles of Tahrir Square. Nevertheless, US troops empower and protect the new Saddamists of the so-called democracy who repress dissent with detainments and torture.
>
> The US government and CNN bless the uprisings of Libya and Syria, while ignoring Iraqi struggles, as they tell the whole world that Iraqis prosper in the "democracy" that the United States installed. Scenes of one hundred thousand Iraqi rebels on 25 February still echo in our minds. Youths such as Aya led those demonstrations, and may still bring about a final uprising and ousting of a corrupt and oppressive government and a never-ending occupation.

Yanar Mohammed

10 | Message of Solidarity to Occupy Wall Street from the Organization of Women's Freedom in Iraq (OWFI)[37]
3 November 2011

Dear Occupy Wall Street,

The people of the world are watching you, following your news, and hoping that —rather than just vent your anger and frustration—you achieve all of your dreams.

While democracy should guarantee all people an equal say in the decisions that affect their lives, you find yourselves forced to take to the streets, as politicians and bankers make decisions behind closed doors and hire an army of police to send you back home with nothing.

While a wealthy one percent ravages your jobs, health, and very lives, their focus is always on their banks and not on the welfare and future of the innocent, unsuspecting millions of people. In times of growth, those banks are sustained by your labor, resulting in extravagant luxuries for the small percent of the population while their economic failures and crises deny you basic resources and economic rights.

This is the same one percent that pursued the war on Iraq without hearing the millions who marched—in the United States and around the world—expressing their opposition. While claiming democracy, the one percent builds vast armies to be launched not just against people all over the world, but also within their own borders.

A second wave of global revolutions has begun as the ninety-nine percent— that is, the global working class—rejects the tyranny, marginalization, and poverty which capitalist authoritarian governments force onto billions of us. Despite all claims of representation, capitalist states make the people pay the price of the economic failures of their political systems with unemployment and government cuts, while the banks get bailed out by the same resources that people's toil has created. Avoiding the poverty and starvation of billions is never the concern of these so-called democracies as much as the stability of their own political rule. Moreover, that same one percent recreates the same failing model of "democratic" capitalist political structures in newly invaded countries around the globe.

The so-called democracy of Iraq, created by the Western capitalist states, divides Iraqi oil reserves between the one percent politicians and a massive, newly-built army, which is now well-trained to crush Iraq's Tahrir Square demonstrations (active since 25 February), with live ammunition, torture, and beatings. While ninety-nine percent of Iraqis seethe with anger [and wait] for the right conditions to claim what is theirs, they eagerly follow your progress in occupying Wall Street, as our enemy is one [and the same] whether they are American or Iraqi. [Our] enemy is the one percent of ruthless exploiters.

Although plans of US withdrawal from Iraq have been publicized worldwide, we are certain that US bases will remain around our cities and villages in one form or another, fully ready to attack and crush any popular uprising, whenever deemed necessary. Although the US administration has already installed Iraqis to maintain systems of inequality and suppression in Iraq, they will continue to keep their military arsenals on full guard for a worst-case scenario. This is what our newly installed democracy grants us: poverty, inequality, suppression of dissent, and a lack of civil liberties for the vast majority of the people, especially women. People of the world have come to refuse a culture of wars and also the "democracy" of the rich. It is time for a political system of equal wealth for all, in other words, a socialist system, where free market rules cannot starve billions while filling the pockets of a few. Connecting such a movement globally was beyond even the wildest dreams of most visionaries, but has proven to be within reach in 2011. And your #Occupy movement has played a leading role in igniting it.

While hunger and wars are planned and organized by a ruthless one percent, it is the responsibility of the ninety-nine percent to create a better world, built on values of humanity, equality, and prosperity for all. In this world, decision-making will not be taken by World Banks, capitalists, and their representative statesmen, but by the immediate representatives of the working class.

Putting demands to the one percent is not the solution, as they have failed repeatedly and can only proceed with their methods of starving working people and bringing on more economic failures. The time has come for a second step. After occupying the street, it is time to break into the castles and palaces of the one percent, and claim what is rightfully yours, to start a new era based on global peace, equal division of wealth, and humanity.

We stand behind you and carry on our continuous resistance to the rule of the one percent in Iraq, Syria, Egypt, Tunisia, Yemen, and the entire world.

Long live the struggles of the ninety-nine percent, and down with the one percent!

Yanar Mohammed
President, Organization of Women's Freedom in Iraq
31 October 2011

11 | The "Friday of Occupation's Defeat": Celebration, Vigilance, and a New Front
9 December 2011

As the US military withdrawal from Iraq approaches its deadline of 31 December 2011, the Popular Movement to Save Iraq's Uday al-Zaidi released a provocative new statement.[38]

The statement—addressed to the Iraqi and Arab media and signed by fifteen other Iraq-based grassroots organizations—states:

> The day of the US military occupation's defeat by the great Iraqi people and its resistance draws near, and Iraqis have been preparing themselves for a Friday which will be the final chance for those who are anti-occupation to record their name in the history of Iraq's resistance. The day of 30 December 2011, will be called the "Friday of Occupation's Defeat."

The statement goes on: "[That day] the youth will remain in the streets calling for the departure of every last US soldier, under whatever terms or form that the occupation government might adopt." They have also chosen this day "to prepare to open up a new front to resist the second face of the occupation represented by its sectarian government and its divisive constitution, and to resist Iranian influence, which may be considered worse than the US occupation by every measure."

It concludes by calling journalists in the free media to "stand with the [Iraqi] people [. . .] at the doorstep of an important and delicate moment in Iraqi history" and refers to an earlier statement that lists the names and phone numbers of dozens of organizers all over Iraq, who are mobilizing with the coordinating committees for 30 December.

Take it away, free media.

[*See appendix II for list of media contacts published by the Popular Movement to Save Iraq.*]

12│ On the Recent Events in Mosul and Other Cities in Iraq
Falah Alwan
15 June 2014

Mosul and other cities in Iraq are experiencing dramatic, dangerous, and fateful changes.

The media, especially that which is allied with the Iraqi government and Western states, has been focusing on the Islamic State (IS) and its control over several Iraqi cities, provoking its audiences against the militant group. Indeed, IS terrorist groupings do exist among armed groups there and its influence in the recent events is clear. However, it is also true that Iraqis generally reject IS, whether in the central or southern regions of Iraq or in parts of the country that are no longer under government control: the so-called "Sunni" areas or the "Sunni Triangle," a term that intelligence services, particularly the US Central Intelligence Agency (CIA), devised as part of a plan to engineer sectarianism in Iraq. At the same time, Iraqis generally reject Maliki's regime and its policies, built as they are on an ethno-sectarian basis. This is especially the case in urban areas where sectarian discrimination is most concentrated, wherein the government treats ordinary people as political enemies.

The fall of several Iraqi cities in the hands of armed groups does not represent the dreams of the people who live there. Their demands to be rid of sectarianism are clear and direct. They expressed them through nonviolent sit-ins, but armed terrorist groups took advantage of this environment to take power. The people's demands against discrimination and sectarianism are just and fair, whereas Maliki's policies are reactionary and discriminatory, and are therefore rejected. In the meantime, the Islamic State's control of cities and people poses a serious threat to everyday life and to society.

Popular demands have morphed into a tool for reactionary forces to divide up the political pie, from the terrorists of al-Qa'ida, the Ba'th Party, and tribal leaders to the Shi'i religious leadership that has called for open warfare and the Kurdish nationalist forces that have achieved military and political gains. This all comes at a moment when Iraq has clearly become divided according to the wills of dominant political forces, whereas the will of the Iraqi people remains ignored.

Regional forces that benefit from Iraq's disintegration—especially Iran, Saudi Arabia, and Turkey—operate in their own way to achieve political gains. All the while the US government—the prime cause of these problems to begin with—prepares to intervene however it chooses. President Obama has so far expressed his concern over Iraqi oil twice when talking about recent events. He has not shown any regard or concern for the fate of two million people now under the control of IS, or for the women who have started committing suicide in Mosul as a result of IS gangs. The working class in Iraq is the common force that exists across the county, from the north of Kurdistan to the furthest points south. It is this force whose very existence and survival depends on the eradication of discrimination and the unification of the Iraqi people. This is the only force that can end fragmentation and division.

We reject US intervention and protest President Obama's inappropriate speech in which he expressed concern over oil and not over people. We also stand firmly against the brazen meddling of Iran.

We stand against the intervention of Gulf regimes and their funding of armed groups, especially Saudi Arabia and Qatar.

We reject Nouri al-Maliki's sectarian and reactionary policies.

We also reject armed terrorist gangs and militias' control of Mosul and other cities. We agree with and support the demands of people in these cities against discrimination and sectarianism.

Finally, we reject the interference of the religious institution and its call for indiscriminate warfare.

We aim to stand with those who represent the interests of the people and to empower them in the face of this dangerous and reactionary attack. We call for a clear international position to curb the deteriorating situation as well as regional interference, and to support the people of Iraq.

Falah Alwan
Federation of Workers' Councils and Unions in Iraq

[This statement was translated from Arabic by Ali Issa.]

SECTION II
Interviews

13 | Iraq After Maliki's "100 Days": An Interview with Uday al-Zaidi[39]
9 June 2011

On 27 February 2011, Iraqi prime minister Nouri al-Maliki gave his parliament one hundred days to "reform" their often nonfunctional ministries or face consequences, in response "to people's demands," as he put it. Those demands have taken the form of some of the least noted events of the Arab uprisings, such as large mobilizations in Baghdad's Tahrir Square; mass acts of civil disobedience and a general strike in Mosul; and the resignations of several governors all over Iraq, including two Basra governors. The Iraqi government has responded violently, with curfews, live ammunition, and wide scale arrests, which prompted Iraqis to call 18 March the "Friday of Prisoners." That deadline for reform ended on 7 June, and many Iraqi civil society leaders—such as Uday al-Zaidi, head of the Popular Movement to Save Iraq—are preparing for renewed protests this summer, calling Friday, 10 June, the "Friday of Resolution and Departure."

The past three months have also seen a large shift in Maliki's position on the presence of US troops in Iraq. Maliki shifted from insisting on their scheduled withdrawal at the end of 2011 to allowing for the possibility of a new agreement, which would extend their stay after approval by a "national referendum." Iraqis have been discussing at length what they see as the present Iraqi government's double crisis of legitimacy: an utter lack of the ability to provide the most basic services as well as obedience to a deeply unpopular military occupation and regional forces. Meanwhile, grassroots organizers saw this as an opportunity to make their protests have a real impact. In the following interview, Zaidi discusses his brothers, what he thinks has been driving these protests, who is participating, and what he sees as the most prominent demands. The interview was conducted and translated on 25 May 2011.

Ali Issa [AI]: Could you introduce yourself? Where are you from in Iraq? What is your profession outside of your political activism?

Uday al-Zaidi [UZ]: I was born in Baghdad but [my family] is originally from the south of Iraq, in Dhi Qar Province. I was employed at the Ministry of Culture, and was fired from my job when my brother threw shoes at President George W. Bush. I now lead the Popular Movement to Save Iraq, which is a popular, youth-led organization from within Iraq. Its demands are the end of the occupation, the liberation of Iraq, and the removal of corrupt agents that came in on the backs of tanks. In addition, we seek to put a stop to the powerful Iranian forces in the country—liberating Iraq from Iranian influence.

AI: Your two brothers Muntazar and Thurgham have joined you in speaking out against both the occupation and Maliki's regime. Is there a particular reason the Zaidi family has been so involved in organizing?

UZ: The Zaidi family is like any other family in Iraq, a working-class family. Our love of Iraq is what drove us. But we took advantage of the fact that people knew us after my brother Muntazar threw shoes at the criminal Bush, and we wanted to raise the issue of what was happening in Iraq. So we started organizing all over Iraq, the south, the center, and the north. We took advantage of people's affection for us to work for the sake of Iraq as a whole. We founded the organization [Popular Movement to Save Iraq], and thank God, it is now active from the north to the south.

AI: When did the mass protests begin in Iraq?

UZ: People might be surprised to learn that the sit-ins and protests in Iraq started before the ones in Tunisia. The Popular Movement [to Save Iraq] and other youth organizations had been readying themselves and coming out to sizable protests, especially in the western and northern regions [of Iraq] and somewhat in the south. Some might recall the protest that happened in Basra in June 2010, which was quite large and resulted in the governor of Basra stepping down. So these protests did not begin after what has been called the "Arab Spring" of revolution, but actually preceded it. We came out with our demands before Tunisia, Egypt, and Yemen because we are an occupied country. We languish under two occupations: a US and an Iranian occupation, as well as their agents, the corrupt politicians in Iraq. That is why at first these protests were dominated by youth, but now people from all sectors of society have come out—youth, children, elders, women, and men, without exception. Very soon, God willing, after the period of one hundred days which Maliki set for himself [to address the protesters' demands], there is going to be a mass sit-in which we expect will cover Iraq from the south to the north. Three days ago, a sit-in began in Dhi Qar Province and will continue, and hopefully, 7-10 June will be the end of Iraq's present period, the reign of the occupation and its enablers.

AI: The governor of Basra resigned on 25 February, after large demonstrations there called for his removal. Have there been other resignations of this kind? What is their significance?

UZ: Sure. The organizations in the coalition, and if I could mention some of their names, since many of the individuals prefer to remain anonymous, are, for example: the Movement to Liberate the South, the Popular Movement to Save Kirkuk, the Organization of Students of a Free Iraq, the National Organization of Tribal Leaders of the South and the Central Euphrates, the Movement of Rising Iraqis, the Coalition to Support the Iraqi Revolution, and the Movement of Iraqi Youth. All these organizations and some coalitions—like the February 25 Coalition and the Great Iraqi Revolution—are preparing for a day called the "Day of Retribution," from 7-10 June. As for the governor of Basra, in addition to the governor of Kut who ran away, and the governors of Dhi Qar and Salah al-Din before that, we are not focused on them. They do not really factor into the calculations of the United States and its agents. Our target is the top of the pyramid, Prime Minister Nouri al-Maliki, and the members of his parliament, which was formed on the basis of a sectarian quota system. In Iraq, we have a prime minister that must be Shi'i, the president must be Kurdish, and [the] speaker of the parliament must be Sunni. We want an end and revocation of this sectarian quota system. We have no problem with the president or the speaker, whatever their religious or ethnic background, as long as they are Iraqi.

AI: Have your demands ever contained matters related to oil or economic sovereignty?

UZ: As you know, when the US occupation forces invaded Iraq, they did so under the claim that Saddam Hussein had weapons of mass destruction (WMDs). When they occupied Iraq, the justification changed to protecting civilians. Yet, Western forces, which include the US military, are now targeting civilians in Libya and other parts of the world. Oil was not the prime factor that brought occupation forces to Iraq. If you want to know about Iraqi resources that play a role in [the] game the occupation is playing: there is mercury in the south, and phosphate, tin, flint, and even uranium in Sumawah Province. These are minerals that the United States needs because, along with Europe and parts of eastern Asia, it has run out of them. As for oil, when we go out to protest and demand the fall of the Iraqi client regime, it is not a power grab. We have the following communiqué, if you would allow me to read it, so you can understand our movement's principles:

And there is life for you in retaliation, O men of
understanding, that you may guard yourselves.
Quran 2:179, *Surat al-Baqara*

To the people of Iraq everywhere: The date ending the period
of Maliki's one hundred days that he set for himself and his
government draws near, but we admit that we were not really
waiting, and did not hold out during this time. We were
organizing actions with other organizations before and during
the countdown to 7 June. But the ending of the hundred day
period, with no achievement whatsoever, was the fuse we were
waiting for, for those who were giving Maliki a chance, and
were waiting for reforms from him, his government and
corrupt parliament, [we ask them] to come out and
demonstrate with us.

All those who believed that reform could come from those
corrupt agents have been disappointed. Maliki did not take
advantage of this opportunity, and did not enact reforms or
amendments or improve social services. Services are still going
from bad to worse, security and safety have gone, never to
return, and the stench of treachery has spread. That is why
your brothers at the Popular Movement to Save Iraq and
organizations in coalition, after relying on God, and the best of
this wronged nation, have decided to organize sit-ins all over
Iraq, and are not returning to our homes until Maliki steps
down, the occupation leaves, corrupt politicians are held
accountable, face trial, and the parliament is disbanded. We
demand the formation of a transitional government of
technocrats that can run the country for a temporary period,
and after a period of no more than six months, will set up
transparent elections without regional or outside interference.
The Popular Movement to Save Iraq and other organizations in
coalition have decided not to enter into this transitional
government, and limit our work to organizing sit-ins and
demonstrations only, to bring down the occupation
government, success through God.

This indicates that we are not after power or money. We want what is
positive for our country. We want dignity. When the protests began in Baghdad,

we were not asking for electricity or government subsidies. Some say that these protesters are looking for work, or job opportunities. They are wrong. We are a country that has lost its dignity and freedom. We are not calling for a share of the oil, or for oil to go into this or that sector. Certainly, the oil is the property of Iraq [and] its people, but our foremost concern is the departure of the occupation and its agents from Iraq. We will take on these issues in due time.

14 | On the Ground in Basra: An Interview with Hashmeya Muhsin al-Saadawi
2 May 2012

Iraqi unions demonstrated on May Day 2012 at a difficult historical moment. Still operating without a labor law that sanctions their organizing and under the consolidation of Prime Minister Nouri al-Maliki's growing police/military powers, their movement faces an array of antagonistic forces. In this wide-ranging discussion, Basra-based Hashmeya Muhsin al-Saadawi, president of the Electrical Utility Workers Union in Iraq and the first female vice president of the General Federation of Iraqi Workers in Basra, discusses Iraqi security after the US withdrawal, the legacy of the US occupation, the sectarian quota system, the state of union organizing, electricity, and the Iraqi protest movement—one of the least covered of the Arab uprisings. She also discusses the important struggle in 2006 and 2007 over the Iraq Hydrocarbon Law. This was a law that aimed, among other things, to remove parliamentary oversight over government decisions on energy contracts with multinational corporations. The Iraqi government and occupying forces pushed hard to make this law pass, but Iraqi civil society ultimately defeated it.

Ali Issa (AI): Has the withdrawal of official US forces changed Iraq's security situation on the ground?

Hashmeya Muhsin al-Saadawi (HS): To answer that question, let me start with 31 August 2010, because it was an important step in ending the occupation and regaining sovereignty, according to the timetable included in the withdrawal agreement signed by Iraq and the United States. On that day, US forces completed their withdrawal from cities, and their mission shifted to training Iraqi forces. Complete withdrawal was then realized on 31 December 2011, leaving behind very few troops whose sole mandate was to "provide training."

Iraqi security and military forces are still facing problems, including not being adequately trained, which goes back to a few causes, among them that some Iraqi political forces did not want a US withdrawal. There is also the fact that the sectarian quota system is reflected even within the structure of the Iraqi armed forces, which should recruit members based on professionalism, skills, and patriotism, and not loyalty to a party or sect.

The deterioration of the political situation since 2007 repeatedly tabling serious decisions, the weakness of the Council of Representatives [*majlis al-*

nuwwab], in-fighting between dominant blocs, and the deadlock that now governs the relationship between them all have had negative effects on the strength of the security forces and their role during these difficult and sensitive times.

AI: Are there Iraqi demands with regard to the responsibility of the US government, which was the driving force of the occupation?

HS: Iraqis lived under a repressive, all-encompassing dictator for over three decades. That regime brought great suffering to Iraq and the entire region. I do not want to get into this because it has become clear to the whole world—*now* it is clear to the world, after it had been deaf and blind to Saddam and his agents' oppression and torture of Iraqis. We wanted to get rid of this regime, but not through war and occupation. Because all the occupation did was bring new pain, including destroying what was left of the country's infrastructure, the undoing of its institutions, and opening its borders to killers, terrorists, and weapons dealers. In addition, the occupation planted the seeds of sectarianism from which thousands of Iraqis have died. Now the occupation is leaving after it has finished its mission and got what it came for. The occupation is the main party responsible for Iraq's destruction, but we do not really imagine for one minute that the US government will help with the true crises we have on many levels. So there is no way out except for serious and responsible efforts of political forces in Iraq, both those who are in power and outside of it, to reassess deeply the political process and the sectarian quota system on which it is based. Reform of that process, and getting it on the right track, could allow us to build a civil, democratic, united country.

AI: The union movement in Iraq has faced great challenges from successive Iraqi governments and the occupation since 2003, like the maintenance of Saddam Hussein's 1987 law that criminalized independent union organizing. But despite these challenges, sectors of that movement were able to launch a successful and populist campaign against the oil and gas law from 2006 to 2009. What are the movement's greatest challenges now?

HS: Under the past regime, there was no union organizing in the public sector due to the terrible Labor Law 150 of 1987. After that regime fell, the workers quickly put together unions in the public sector, worked very hard, but faced many agendas the US occupation brought with it. The occupation launched several consecutive attacks against the union movement: the occupation forces' attacks on the Baghdad headquarters of the General Federation of Trade Unions in Iraq; the parliamentary Order 8750 in 2005 that froze the accounts of that federation; and the ferocious attack on the oil and electricity unions that opened the door to anyone unionizing in the public sector being charged under article 4(2) of the Anti-Terrorism Law.

The union movement challenged the oil and gas law project and launched a campaign, aided by patriotic forces, Iraqi academics, and international labor allies that revealed the faults with this law, chief among them its lack of parliamentary oversight with regard to contracts with multinationals. We are not against the passing of a law that safeguards the rights of the people, protects our oil wealth, and reinforces the role of the Iraq National Oil Company [Iraq's public oil company which has been government owned since 1972].

At the same time, the General Federation of Trade Unions in Iraq launched a campaign to pass a labor law that is fair for workers and that matches work standards and international agreements. A proposal for this law was introduced in 2005, and the parliament and the government are still dragging their feet and tinkering with it. They have removed key parts, including not explicitly extending the law to the protections for organizing in the public sector as well as deleting the section on protections for non-union workers. They watered it down to the point that it no longer meets international labor standards as set by the International Labor Organization in 1919.

Relying on constitutional rights, the electrical worker unions in Basra recently launched a campaign called "Social Security is the Right of Every Iraqi," which is supported by some international friends, the Federation of Unions in Holland being one of them.

AI: What is the situation with electricity like on the ground?

HS: The issue of electricity has remained a daily battle, a bitter reality that has become great fodder for sarcasm. It bears mentioning the infrastructure problems that Saddam's regime caused—with its foolish policies and destructive wars—and the subsequent terrorist attacks that have targeted generators and grids, such as the wave of bombings that hit transmission towers and electrical import lines on 7 December 2011. Most recently, there has been a gross exaggeration of how much money the government has spent on this sector with no tangible results after their promises of improvement.

The Ministry of Electricity had promised a minimum of ten hours a day throughout Iraq once the needs of state health and security institutions have been met. In reality, people get between four to six hours of electricity a day, with some houses getting no power whatsoever for a full day or even several days.

The Ministry of Finance estimates that twenty-seven billion dollars in public funds have been spent on electricity since 2003. Yet, the Ministry of Electricity has failed to rebuild this sector, a failure that has been compounded by the security factor, which includes attacks such as the above mentioned 7 December terrorist attacks. This is partly due to the lack of consultation with Iraqi experts who know what they are doing as well as mismanagement and widespread corruption. Now, just like every spring, officials appear on television and start making their brittle and hilarious promises, with some unionists joking that we might be exporting electricity to our neighbors or even Europe!

AI: What is your opinion of the Arab uprising-style movement in Iraq that started on 25 February 2011 and has been called by some the "forgotten uprising"? Did unions participate in the mobilizations, given that the latter have recently gotten smaller in number? [40] Finally, do you have any explanation for the lack of media coverage, even in the Arabic-language media?

HS: Iraq has seen successive waves of sit-ins, demonstrations, and protest activities. They have been the result of the continued hardships in daily life and the lack of basic services as well as the deterioration of security since April 2003 that I described. On top of all that, there have been major efforts to limit civil liberties and silence people while cementing the hated ethno-sectarian quota system. We consider all this an open and direct violation of the constitution. Many sectors of society have participated in these protests: youths, women, civil society groups, unions, and the newer pro-democracy formations.

The right of citizens to demonstrate, express opinions, and take political positions is a constitutional right, and the government and its apparatuses should provide the necessary amount of security to whoever is exercising this right. The government should listen closely to people's legal demands and seek to satisfy them. It should also pay attention to popular calls for the reform of the political process and correct its course on the path to building a civil, democratic state, based on the text of the constitution that citizens voted for in October 2005.

It should be obvious that our Iraq is not isolated from what is happening in the countries of the region, though it might differ in its internal dynamics and specificities. The storms of change around us have also energized our people to break the wall of silence and to take to the streets. The role of the youth, who have taken advantage of new social media technology, has been key in this movement.

But the way the Iraqi government and its apparatuses have treated the protest movements is a serious violation of the constitutional right to freedom of expression and peaceful protest, and an attempt to stifle the practice of that right. That is when the people understood that the first and last concern of influential ruling political blocs is to look after their own interests, struggle with each other over power, and divide the pie among themselves, without any regard for ordinary people living under cruel conditions in a country whose yearly budget exceeds one hundred billion dollars.

The protests of 25 February 2011, as well as the mobilizing that led to these protests and emerged from them, were a great success. They expressed the clear and just demands of the people, despite government attempts to distort the depth of the movement and its goals. For example, at times, the Iraqi government labeled the protesters "rioters," and at others, it claimed that "more jobs" was their sole demand. Then there has been the intrusion of the prime minister's cabinet, with all its influence, to try to stop the movement, the attempts of the government as a whole to abort it, and all the surveillance and incarceration that followed.

Whether the protests will resume depends on the reasons that lead to their eruption. To this day, none of the protesters' demands have been met, so if the government continues on its present path, disregarding people's rights and needs, it is very likely the protests will return.

As for media coverage, initially there had been coverage from several television stations, but the government put pressure on them and shut down some of their offices. In addition, a good number of journalists were beaten by infiltrators at the protests—thugs—while others were arrested and detained. The assassination of journalists—those brave, honorable people—including the writer and poet Hadi al-Mahdi, has also exacerbated this tragic situation.

15│ The Unfinished Story of Iraq's Oil Law: An Interview with Greg Muttitt
24 July 2012

"No Blood for Oil" was a slogan featured on many signs in demonstrations during the run-up to the US-led invasion of Iraq in 2003 and throughout the early years of the occupation as global opposition to it grew. But as Iraq faded from the headlines in 2009, the struggle over its oil continued. In the following interview, Greg Muttitt, investigative journalist and author of the groundbreaking Fuel on the Fire: Oil and Politics in Occupied Iraq *(2012), discusses the attempts by occupying forces, multinational oil giants, and newly minted Iraqi "leaders" to privatize Iraq's oil.[41] Having worked directly with Iraq's oil unions, Muttitt also describes the heroic role that Iraqi civil society played in challenging these efforts, how it all panned out, and where it might be headed today, at an especially sensitive moment when the Iraqi labor movement is facing a series of fresh attacks.[42]*

Ali Issa (AI): Based on the hundreds of US/UK government documents you have unearthed through Freedom of Information Act requests, what were your findings about the role of oil in the 2003 Iraq War?

Greg Muttitt (GM): Unsurprisingly, the documentary record shows that oil was a central part of the strategic thinking behind the war, and consistently shaped the conduct of the occupation. My book is primarily about what happened during the occupation. The United States, the United Kingdom, and the international community were keen to see Iraq's oil developed through foreign investment. It was not so much about helping out their own corporations—that was a secondary concern for them. What they wanted was to see foreign investment in Iraq as a starting point for opening up the other nationalized industries, especially in the region, so as to get oil flowing more quickly. Iraq's oil sector had been nationalized since the 1970s. The nationalization took place mostly in 1972, and its final phases continued until 1975. Essentially, what they wanted to do was to reverse that: put multinational oil companies back in the dominant role in the Iraqi oil sector.

AI: You place the struggle over Iraq's oil law at the center of Iraq's recent history. What is the oil law, how has it evolved, and what is its present status?

GM: The first post-Saddam permanent government drafted the oil law in 2006. Then the Bush administration pushed it especially hard through 2007. The law had three purposes. The first was to create a framework in which multinationals would have a primary role in developing Iraq's oil industry, and to determine exactly the extent of that role, what rights they would have, and the extent of their powers. The second element was to clarify how that would work in an emerging federal system in Iraq. To put it simply: With whom would multinationals sign contracts? Would it be with the central government in Baghdad, or with regional governments—in particular, the only one that exists so far, the Kurdistan Regional Government?

The third element of the law was to essentially disempower parliament in relation to decisions around oil. Iraq's 1967 Law No. 97, which stated that if the government were to sign contracts to develop oil fields and run them, the parliament would have to sign a specific piece of legislation to approve them. In other words, the parliament would have to say, "We support and agree with this contract and we give it validity in law." That was still in force in 2003, and indeed in 2006. The government could legally sign contracts with foreign companies. But if it did so, it would have to get approval from parliament for the contracts to have any force. Therefore, the most important role of the oil law of 2006/2007 was not so much to allow contracts to be signed by multinationals, as that was already possible. It was to allow the contracts to be signed without parliament having any oversight. Incidentally, the importance of parliamentary oversight is that oil accounts for over ninety-five percent of government revenue. So it is quite reasonable for parliament to have some say in how that works.

So this was the oil law. The United States, the United Kingdom, the International Monetary Fund (IMF), and other financial institutions wanted it passed as soon as the permanent post-Saddam government was formed in May 2006. As soon as that happened, the United States and the United Kingdom started to say, "Your priority is going to be to pass the oil law." I have documents from that period that make this very clear. The Iraqi government moved very quickly to draft an oil law in August 2006, and it basically delivered those three elements. Getting this law passed in parliament became the major political priority of the United States.

AI: But the law did not pass. What prevented its passage?

GM: There were two barriers to it passing. First, there were disputes between Iraq's politicians—primarily, between Kurdish politicians and everyone else. The dispute was over the degree of decentralization. Essentially, it was a squabble between politicians who thought only about their own interests, their ethno-sectarian groups' interests, or which of them would get the right to sign contracts and thereby control revenues. This dispute over decentralization slowed down the law's progress, and people on either side of that debate leaked the draft law to their allies.

This led to the second factor, which was the Iraqi population's overwhelming opposition to giving multinationals such a central role. I think those in the US administration and the Iraqi government knew this. So the way they planned to deal with it was by not telling anyone that this oil law was going through. But it was leaked in October 2006. Although there were two barriers the media only recognized the first: the squabbling of politicians.

Once the draft law was leaked, knowledge of the law started to spread to civil society. In December 2006, I attended a meeting of Iraq's trade unions in Amman. They were discussing the law and decided that they were going to campaign against it. Their strategy, which began in early 2007, was basically just to get the law known: to tell people about it. So they produced pamphlets, which they handed out to their members and to the general public. They also organized conferences, public meetings, demonstrations, etc. The more this was done, the more people knew about it, and the more anger there was that in secret this government, which had a fairly limited mandate given the circumstances of an election under occupation, was trying to push something that the occupation powers were demanding. This would do considerable damage to Iraqi interests and the Iraqi economy. Iraqis feel very strongly that oil should remain in Iraqi hands, not least because of their historical experience with foreign companies. So, during the course of 2007, this opposition spread. One after another, new groups and new constituencies got involved.

AI: What did the Bush administration do?

GM: At the same time that opposition to the oil law was spreading through the first half of 2007, the Bush administration ramped up the pressure on the Iraqi parliament to get it passed. The administration was very frustrated and angry that it had not been passed at the end of 2006. All the while, they claimed publicly that it was the dispute with the Kurds over decentralization that was holding things up. The Bush administration then claimed that the law was about the sharing of revenues between different groups, which it was not at all.

The surge, which was announced in January 2007 and sent an extra thirty thousand troops to Iraq, was very clearly one side of a two-part strategy. You can read this in the documents published by the Bush administration at the time. It was called "The New Way Forward," and its two parts were to send thirty thousand troops to control and pacify the country, and to use that control delivered by the extra military force to push Iraqi politicians to deliver what they called benchmarks—markers of political progress. By far the foremost among these was passing the oil law. It was all they ever talked about. In meetings with members of the Maliki government, US administration officials kept saying, "When are you going to pass the oil law? Where is our oil law?"

During this period, there were also very strong indications from the US military that if the oil law was not passed, the Maliki government would no longer have the support of the United States. Maliki very clearly understood it as a threat to remove him from power. So, through the course of 2007, the pressure was increasing on both sides. On one side, Iraqi civil society exerted great pressure. This was started by the trade unions but spread into broader civil society—religious and secular as well as the professionals who had run the oil industries since nationalization. They were all saying, "This oil law is bad news for Iraq, do not pass it." On the other side, you had the Bush administration applying more and more pressure to get the law passed.

AI: What was the outcome?

GM: The popular opposition to the oil law grew so great that it started to spread to parliament. Members of the Iraqi parliament started to see a political opportunity in opposing the oil law, and a political threat in supporting it—a threat to their future political careers. By July 2007, the majority of the Iraqi parliament was against it. The US administration had set September 2007 as the deadline for passing the oil law, and this was when General David Petraeus and Ambassador Ryan Crocker were going to report to Congress on how the surge was going. They were very clearly saying to the Iraqi government, "Give us the benchmarks, give us the oil law by September, otherwise you will face all of these consequences that we warned you of." But by that stage it was a majority of the parliament that was against the oil law; they could not therefore get the oil law approved by parliament. The September deadline arrived, and there was no oil law. Today there is still no oil law.

To me that is quite a remarkable story, and it is an untold story. It is remarkable in that Iraqi civil society was able to prevent the United States from getting this vital objective, in which they had invested so much political capital, simply through talking about it. It was partly a measure of the distance between what the United States was demanding—and absolutely desperately wanted— and what the vast majority of Iraqis passionately felt should happen. After investing all that political capital, the US government failed to pass the oil law. September 2007, therefore, marked the beginning of the decline of US influence in Iraq. We saw that much more clearly through the course of 2008, in particular the failure to get a deal that would keep US troops [in Iraq] indefinitely, since the status of forces agreement had a three-year term limit. But I think it was this moment that marked the shift in Iraqi politics from being absolutely dominated by the United States to having a rising Iraqi voice.

AI: Why then are multinational oil companies in Iraq now?

GM: In the latter half of 2009, the Iraqi government awarded several contracts to foreign companies—British Petroleum (BP), Shell, Exxon, and so on—even without the oil law, and without showing the contracts to parliament. They are a hybrid form of contract, not the production sharing agreements the companies really wanted. Importantly, they are technically illegal and have not been approved by parliament since Law No. 97 is still in force.

AI: The challenge to the oil law succeeded, so the contracts could be declared illegal in a future Iraqi government. What are the conditions necessary for a second challenge, a second wave to come up against the contracts that have been signed?

GM: After the first contracts were signed in 2009, there was a member of the Iraqi parliament, Shatha al-Musawi, who challenged the first of the contracts, which was with BP, in the Iraqi Supreme Court. Her challenge was unsuccessful, but not on substantive legal grounds. Rather, it was stopped on process grounds and bureaucratic bottlenecks. In others words, it was held up and bypassed through subcommittees. The Supreme Court has been quite problematic over the last few years because Maliki's government has had increasing influence over its decisions, and that has been seen in a number of decisions that have gone the way Maliki wanted them to, in contradiction to where the written law should have pushed it. This influence was seen especially after the 2010 election when the Supreme Court gave Maliki the right to form the government over Ayad Allawi. There are strong indications that Maliki has channels of influence. In the case of Shatha al-Musawi's challenge to the BP contract, the court ordered her to pay a refundable deposit of three hundred million Iraqi dinars, which was about two hundred and twenty-five thousand dollars at the time. She would get her money back only if she won the case. She did not have that kind of money, so the case collapsed.

So, in order to carry out a legal challenge in Iraq, I think there would need to be some means of containing government influence over the Supreme Court. A way of containment might be a set of institutions that financially, institutionally, and politically support the case, such that it becomes difficult for the Maliki government to steer the court or for the court to side with the government. But that is the major obstacle there. I think, however, that such a challenge could also come from the government itself. Traditionally, challenges to contracts come from the governments of oil-producing countries. A government says, this is not in our interest, we are going to change the terms, or we are even going to cancel it. This has happened a lot over the past decade around the world. Now, companies use legal mechanisms in the contracts to prevent governments from doing that—to get the contracts judicable in international investment tribunals, rather than in the courts of individual countries.

The fact is that these contracts are not validated within Iraqi law. That Iraqi law requires parliamentary approval, and parliamentary approval has not been sought [out] or given, means that a future Iraqi government can change the terms of the contracts or even tear them up. Further, if the companies concerned went to an investment tribunal in Europe or in the United States, the government could argue, and I believe it would have a very strong case, that these contracts are not legal. The government could argue that the Law No. 97 of 1967 is still in force, and it requires parliamentary approval. In short, if approval is not sought out, the contracts are void. Now the conditions for that to happen would be a government that believed there was a problem with the contracts, and probably it means a different government from the current one. It would be politically embarrassing, to say the least, for the current government to argue that the contracts are illegal on the basis of what this same government did not do—i.e., take it to parliament. So a change in the government could drive this.

But Iraqi politics strikes me as very fluid at the moment. I could not predict what the nature of the Iraqi political system will be in a year's time. I think it is hard to say whether Maliki will still be there; it is more likely that he will, but I would not put a great deal of money on it.

AI: In their rejection of the oil law, did you get a sense for what unions and civil society were hoping for? Are their visions much like those for nationalization of oil in pre-1990 Iraq, or do they differ?

GM: When you look at the history of the Iraqi oil industry, the most successful period, of which Iraqis in the oil sector field are very proud, is the period immediately after nationalization. So from 1972 to 1979, for instance, production increased from one and a half million barrels a day to three and a half million . . . They were finding greater quantities of reserves there each year than in the rest of the world. What I heard, especially from the senior managers and technicians in the oil industry, was that if you want to run a technically successful oil industry in Iraq—and that was what they were interested in since they were technocrats—then the way to do it is to keep it in the public sector. The only reason you would privatize it and bring in foreign companies is for ideological reasons.

I think the only problem with keeping the oil industry in the public sector was that Iraq was behind on technology as a result of the sanctions period. But many people recognize that technology is something you can buy. You can hire a company like Schlumberger to come and install some if its new separators, or pumps, or whatever it is. They can install them, they can train the Iraqis how to use them, and they can even operate them for a couple of years until the Iraqis have got the hang of it—quite straightforward. But that is very different from signing a twenty-year contract that gives a company like BP or Exxon control over the oil field and management of it.

There was some debate as to exactly how far the government should go in terms of letting foreign companies in. There were varying degrees of pragmatism towards that. Some said maybe it is OK to have BP for five years. Or maybe it is OK to have BP as long as they are in a junior role. The absolute objection was to the idea of putting a company like BP in control, having the primary management and decision-making role for a long period, like twenty years, especially when there was homegrown Iraqi expertise.

AI: You have argued that the decimation that the sanctions caused triggered a kind of slow rebuilding of the oil industry by many of the technicians who remained, which thereafter created a sense of ownership over that rebuilding. So the other side of the reaction to sanctions seems to have been the maintenance and even strengthening of a national consciousness that then played an important role in Iraqi civil society's response to the oil law.

GM: The way one of the oil workers in Basra put it to me was, we Iraqis have rebuilt our oil industry three times. We rebuilt it in the late 1980s after the war with Iran. We rebuilt it after the Gulf War, and we did so then under sanctions, when it was especially difficult. And we rebuilt it after 2003. Halliburton was getting paid for doing it but essentially doing nothing. We have rebuilt our oil industry three times, and that gives us a sense of ownership over, and belief in, our oil industry. This is something we rebuilt. It is very different from when you pay someone to come in and rebuild it for you. That is not something we will willingly hand over.

16 | Tipping Toward Iraq's Squares: An Interview with Falah Alwan
22 January 2013

The Iraqi state released 335 detainees in January of 2013. Prime Minister Nouri al-Maliki bussed in a few hundred paid "supporters" to rally. What gives? Signs point to the wave of mass anti-government protests mostly around the provinces Anbar, Nineveh, and Salah al-Din, which have shaken Iraq since 21 December 2012. These evolving mobilizations have sometimes brought out numbers approaching hundreds of thousands—as in Mosul's Ahrar Square—and led to the blocking of a major Iraq-Jordan-Syria highway. Some have also claimed the recent mobilizations as an "Iraqi Spring." By 7 January 2013, Iraqi security and pro-government thugs began physically attacking the protesters. The demands—ever a contentious issue given the many layers of influence in Iraq—have focused on releasing Iraq's detained (namely women), ending the casual use of the death penalty, and the closely related issue of combating sectarianism, which lies at the heart of Iraq's many social and political crises.⁴³ In a complex interplay, both civil society and the sectarian political elite have struggled over the meaning of these protests. In particular, they have interpreted the word "equality" very differently—especially as these mobilizations have been centered in areas of Iraq traditionally associated with Sunni populations. These mobilizations garnered more media than the mass protests of early-to-mid 2011, according to blogger Reidar Visser, who pointed out, "International media are attracted to these protests precisely because they fit in a sectarian narrative about a simplistic Sunni-Shi'i battle over Iraq."⁴⁴ How "sectarian" are these protests exactly, and what might be their potential beyond that narrow frame? To get a firmer understanding of the moment's dynamics, I spoke with Baghdad-based Falah Alwan, president of the Federation of Workers' Councils and Unions in Iraq (FWCUI), about what brought this about and where it all may be going.

Ali Issa (AI): What just happened in Iraq to trigger mass mobilizations, given that the street has been very quiet in the past several months?

Falah Alwan (FA): The protests that many Iraqi cities are witnessing now are not actually in reaction to a passing event. That is to say they are not the direct result of some government action. The street that your question describes as "quiet" is actually silent only as a result of repression, especially after the protests of February 2011 when the authorities revealed their violence openly—using the army to clamp down on nonviolent protests and firing live ammunition at peaceful protestors. It may be that a particular event triggered what is happening now, but the content of the protests now goes well beyond the prime minister vs.

the finance minister. You have surely noticed the development of the slogans people are raising. While the "trigger" was the arrest of the finance minister's security guards, the protesters demanded the end of article 4 of Iraq's Anti-Terrorism Law, which authorities have used as an instrument to repress any dissent. They have also used it against all strikes and nonviolent sit-ins that workers demanding their rights have organized for years—especially the protests of the Basra oil workers in 2006-2007. Protesters are also now demanding the end of sectarianism or sectarian discrimination, while others are asking for work opportunities and a remedy to unemployment.

AI: What is the state of prisoners in Iraq now, especially women prisoners? Are there reliable numbers?

FA: With regard to women prisoners, we at FWCUI used to receive field reports from a team at the Organization of Women's Freedom in Iraq (OWFI) that visited women's prisons, and they would report numbers of rape cases and other violations. The consolidation of government control post-2009, especially in the aftermath of the 2011 protests, has made these visits extremely difficult. Also, political, civil society, and feminist groups are absolutely banned from visiting the prisons that hold people for political reasons, under accusations of "terrorism." As for numbers, according to government institutions, there are one thousand women detained, with four thousand arrested and under interrogation. Other media, however, put the numbers at the tens of thousands.

AI: If elite political and sectarian forces inside and around the regime have played a role in the recent protests, how has the street gone beyond those designs? In your opinion, what is the biggest challenge to the movement spreading to the rest of Iraq?

FA: A situation may remain "quiet" for decades but continue to hold within it the elements of an explosion that can be triggered by any event, which is what happened during the Arab uprisings. Tunisia remained under [Zine El Abidine] Ben Ali's repressive regime for decades without us seeing the "elements" of a revolution. The suicide of Mohamed Bouazizi sparked events that led to the revolution that overtook all of Tunisia, then Egypt, and then the Middle East and even beyond.

Not looking at Iraq as a chain of events, but rather seeking the roots, they lie in a political system and the division of a society based on what they call Shi'i, Sunni, Kurdish, Turkmen, and Christian "component parts." The government then says that it does not discriminate between one part and another, and that

"Iraq is one." Then, politicians wrestle over dividing the ministries between political blocs based on ethnicity, each in a team that hates the other, uniting only in their animosity toward Iraqi society. The centralization of power in Shi'i Islamic parties, the spread of corruption in government institutions, and the inability of the authorities to create a broad political frame that can contain all of Iraqi society have led to a general societal disgust. People have expressed these feelings through a series of protests and sit-ins across Iraq, which have preceded the moment we are living now.

All this led to discrimination against large sections of Iraq in the form of policies and actions like arrests, accusing any opposition group of having affiliation with al-Qa'ida or the Ba'th, etc. These then are the bases from which today's movement launched. On the one hand, this movement is expressing, in a direct and practical way, that the sectarian regime cannot lead society under any circumstance. On the other hand, the areas or provinces that the authorities accused of sectarianism or links with al-Qa'ida and the like are now raising slogans that directly threaten the sectarian structure. This is because the regime actually relies on sectarian claims so it may then reproduce itself by "counteracting" a sectarian or pro-Saddam banner.

These regions have broadcast their opposition to sectarianism and put forward broad slogans—some of which are democratic. As this grows it will seriously strike the ethnic discourse of the central government—which I believe will begin to identify itself on another basis in order to sustain its efforts.

The Maliki government victory over the people in February 2011, and then the score settling with its political opponents, resulted in a narrow, top-down regime that only became more and more insular. The present wave may put an end to this tyranny if social forces can develop through it.

AI: How do the protesting forces attempt to go beyond sectarianism?

FA: From the first days, slogans were demanding unity and a rejection of sectarianism and division. Coming about instinctually and organically—calling for brotherhood between Shi'a and Sunni, Arabs and Kurds . . . as if "unity" were a coming together of Shi'a and Sunni. "Unity" is a positive slogan, no doubt, but raising it in this way, I believe, will again reproduce sectarian political tendencies. I feel that putting out a societal understanding of "unity" based on an objective class analysis is a serious political goal that falls on the shoulders of political groups that have a clear understanding of Iraqi society.

AI: What is the relationship between these protests and the labor movement or the political formations that emerged after 25 February 2011, what some call Iraq's "forgotten uprising"?

FA: I already talked about the relationship to 25 February. Now, labor across Iraq —while acknowledging the lack of deep-rooted institutions—has tools of struggle at its disposal. We are talking about a social class that is at the center of events, even if they are not participating clearly and directly *as the working class*, since the political situation and sectarian divisions deeply paralyze the organizing abilities of workers. In the end, the strengthening of any mass democratic movement will improve the climate for direct workers' struggle.

AI: In your opinion, what could truly make this a turning point in Iraqi political life?

FA: This moment could be a crossroads for more than one possibility—all is open now. First, it is possible that these protests could transform into a broad social revolution that changes the political system and builds another. A new socio-political model could develop, one that opposes the model imposed on, and advertised for, the region. The development of the present movement could refresh the revolution in the region as a whole and will not be apart from it— especially if it spreads through progressive forces to the southern and Kurdish regions.

Another possibility is the continuing stubbornness of the government and its success in strengthening sectarianism, and the eventual deterioration of the situation to armed struggle as well as widespread unrest. This may be similar to what took place in Syria and Iraq during 2006 and 2007, now with the lack of a US presence. The regressive forces that risk losing their seats—should this movement grow—could push society in that direction. They could even attempt to officially divide the whole of Iraq.

The third possibility is that the protests remain concentrated in the west and north while the regime's forces remain elsewhere. Then there might be a truce between some of the forces involved in the protests and the authorities, with a gradual shrinking of the movement.

All of these are possible. Though what has been realized now is that the regime is facing a broad mass of people that publicly rejects its policies and boldly raises banners stating so. In other words, the people have intervened in a sphere that the authorities want to monopolize.

17| The Iraq That Is Not There: An Interview with Ahmed Habib
5 November 2013

"Why would I teach my son Arabic, Ali? Iraq is gone, finished." This is what a friend from Iraq now living in the United States told me in the summer of 2013, and I really did not know what to say. Although the specifics of contact with Iraq may differ—it might be about visiting Iraq, talking about it, or about "the region" as a whole—this is not an uncommon sentiment in the Iraqi diaspora. In the context of this widespread feeling of despair, what is shakomako.net, "an independent digital magazine about everything Iraqi," to do? What role can its emphasis on resilience play in a mainstream media landscape that speaks a very different language? Where exactly does this dominant perception of Iraq come from anyway? Finally, how do tired concepts such as "Iraqi fatigue"—whereby mainstream and even "alternative" media feel they have covered Iraq enough—relate to Iraqis' self-erasure, their own reluctance to push for filling that silence?

Enter Iraqi writer Ahmed Habib, who serves on the editorial team of shakomako.net. Habib left Iraq in 1981 and has since lived in Toronto, among other places. Although he has not visited Iraq since 2004, he still calls Baghdad home. I recently met him in New York City where he tried to get to the roots of some of these issues, namely, representations of Iraq in the media and how so many have come to believe that Iraq is forever a sectarian, bombed-out war zone: "gone."

Ali Issa (AI): How did the idea for shakomako.net begin?

Ahmed Habib (AH): Growing up in an Iraqi household in the Gulf, Baghdad was never far. It touched every part of our family life, from the way we spoke and the food we ate to the relationships we built. Even when we moved further from Iraq, across the Atlantic to settle in Toronto, Iraq was still very much present. It formed our identity as a family, embodied our yearning for home and represented our fear of what was in store. It was both a source of strength and a symbol of our displacement. We were neither here nor there. We needed to make sense of our shared experiences, to bridge the gap between us and ourselves. Rare flashpoints when Iraq was in the news made this need even more deeply felt.

Leading up to the first Gulf War in 1991—which put Iraq back on the map so to speak, and profoundly altered the geopolitics of the region—we wanted to understand the changes that were looming ahead. In the buildup to the 2003 war, Iraq was everywhere again. Reminiscent of the media spectacle of Operation Desert Storm, "Iraq" had once again become a buzzword—detached from notions of home and the stories of our childhood. Instead, Iraq came to denote a purely militaristic target for those opportunists in Washington and other global power centers.

It was a rude awakening for a lot of Iraqis in the diaspora. As millions of Iraqis lived in the relative comfort of cities abroad, millions more inside the country were suffering a slow death. The need for a means of reflection and communication among us, one that linked back home, could not have been clearer. Rife with the contradictions of displacement, a group of Iraqi youth who had met in Doha in 2003 decided to create a platform to reclaim Iraq as it existed in the minds of people around the world. An online magazine, shakomako.net was thus born in the diaspora in 2004, and has since gone through several iterations.[45]

The strength of the people of Iraq in the face of a massive and systemic attack that has destroyed the lives of millions of people through war, sanctions, and dictatorship: that was part of *our* story in the diaspora as well. Our e-zine paid homage to the resilience of Iraqis living inside the country, and the experiences of those no longer living there. It was the proverbial answer to the question "*shakomako?*," which means "what's up?" in Iraqi slang.

Since the launch, we have tried to create an accessible space for both Iraqis and those interested in and inspired by Iraq. As such, we hope to feature voices that do not necessarily identify as Iraqi, but that have been fundamentally transformed by the experiences of Iraq. For example, we published a story by Nadia Daar, who spoke about how her political awakening arose in relation to resistance to the 2003 occupation of Iraq.[46] We also actively try and reach out to writers and poets who live inside the country, to bring their stories to a wider audience. Recently, Mohammed Hazem, a young journalist who has lived in Baghdad all his life, wrote a poem that describes the farcical irrelevance of the Iraqi elections to him and others from his generation.[47]

AI: What were the concrete goals of launching the latest version of shakomako.net, launched on 14 March 2013, on the eve of the ten-year anniversary of the US invasion?

AH: The magazine had been dormant for many years. Launching and operating independent media projects that do not rely on advertising or external funding sources is always a challenge to maintain. But that does not mean that they are impossible to conceive of and grow. The development of new web and media tools over the past several years has made self-publishing much more dynamic and accessible. We felt better equipped to re-launch and maintain our magazine in a more sustainable way. We could not let the ten-year anniversary of the occupation of Iraq pass by quietly. One of the messages we want to convey to our readers is that the creation of independent and alternative media spaces, ones that are relevant to our respective communities, is easier than ever, and empowering.

We felt that there was an absence of any kind of substantial analysis on Iraq. All that we were hearing about Iraq either came from a racist over-simplification of the situation—a story of primitive violent Iraqis who have been killing each other for centuries—or an outdated "troops-out-of-Iraq" mantra that did not take into account the multiple layers of the attack on Iraq—the economic sanctions, the legacy of a brutal dictatorship, and regional isolation. More substantially, our identities as Iraqis were being increasingly fragmented. The stories that described us, and aimed to account for our destruction, were being developed along narrow definitions of what and who is Iraqi, and this was being done primarily along sectarian lines.

From day one of the invasion, US administrators of the new Iraq created a government that was divided by sect and ethnicity. The impact of that is felt today, with ministries and political parties identifying themselves according to which sect they pander to, and not by a political program that has any relevance to the deteriorating living conditions in the country. We want the magazine to tackle the pervasive issue of political sectarianism, but also to talk about Iraq through diverse lenses: political analysis, arts and culture, history and memory, and even football.

We want to present an analysis of Iraq that is accessible to people and that reflects the larger dynamics of what is happening there, and not of the trials and tribulations of one sectarian political movement versus the other. We also want to show that Iraq as an entity is not just a word on a news ticker at the bottom of a television screen, but that there are actual people in Iraq. That Iraq is not just a term used to describe a larger imperialist or geopolitical project. Any analysis that does not put people at the forefront can be construed as superficial, simplistic, and at times even racist. It reflects the problematic ways we sometimes construct narratives of the Other, even if the intention is to show solidarity with an oppressed group. The word Iraq has been printed trillions of times, but very rarely does it reflect the human stories of that place. We must therefore resist the notion of turning the history of the destruction of Iraq into a catchphrase like "Don't Iraq Iran."[48] We must engage on a much deeper level. That is why we try to show different layers of what Iraq is, how war and politics affect all aspects of life, such as culture and sports. In all our interviews with football players, for example, that was the one thing they all kept coming back to: how the unraveling world around them was reflected in the game itself, and how football can also be a unifying force in a country that is falling apart.

AI: An important point made in one of shakomako.net's original calls for submission was from a Facebook note that said: "For many organizers, 2003 marked a critical period in the radicalization of political organizing. Millions took to the streets of major cities all across the world to demonstrate against the impending massacre of Iraqis."[49] How then do you read this in the waning of Iraq-associated global activism in subsequent years, around 2008 for example?

AH: It is a real shame the way Iraq has disappeared from political discourse. It has been buried under the rubble of its own destruction. People are too afraid or lazy to sift through it and make linkages between Iraq and other developments in the region and in the world. In 2007-08, Iraq was being ravaged by a civil war that claimed the lives of hundreds of thousands. There was a large influx of refugees into neighboring countries: almost five million Iraqis. The country was unraveling at the seams. People were being confronted with complexities that did not fit into neat analytical cubbyholes. Instead of engaging these complexities, people just switched off. In addition, international solidarity with Iraq was a casualty of the occupation itself. Civil society work around the world is continuously criminalized, undermined, and attacked. Iraq-related activism was no exception.

It was frustrating to witness that. Many of the same people and corporations benefiting from the destruction of Iraq are actively engaged in destroying marginalized communities all over the world. We want people to make these connections. We hope that the magazine can offer a space for people to educate themselves about Iraq, and more importantly, use this information to confront war profiteers in their own communities. We recently published an article about the way the US military propaganda machine specifically targets young black men through their recruitment campaigns. The article came out during a time of concerted resistance in Chicago against gun violence and school closures ordered by none other than Rahm Emanuel, the city's mayor and former senior advisor to presidents Clinton and Obama. This is the very same Rahm Emanuel who repeatedly justified the war on Iraq.[50] The connections are endless and exist in communities all over the world.

AI: Shakomako.net pieces are often framed by the idea that Iraqis have shown and continue to show dignity in the face of destruction, or as the title of a piece by Nidal El Khairy puts it, "Strength in the Face of Fighter Jets." Why has this emphasis been so important and what implications does this framing give for other societies often portrayed as destroyed, such as Afghanistan, Palestine, and Syria?

AH: Societies rarely see themselves as destroyed. They are cognizant of the colossal size of the destruction that surrounds them, but their resilience is what keeps them alive. The notion that an entire people has been destroyed is part and parcel of the dehumanization that drives war and occupation. In Iraq, the level of destruction brought on by decades of war, dictatorship, sanctions, and occupation is larger than life. Living conditions, basic services, and infrastructure are in fact destroyed, but the drive to live and resist remains the true legacy of Iraq. Khairy's piece captures the strength of everyday people in the face of killing machines. It is a story that weaves itself through Afghanistan, Palestine, Syria, and other sites of tremendous violence and death.

AI: What is next for shakomako.net?

AH: We are a very small publication run by a group of volunteers and we are always looking to widen our circle and engage more people, whether as contributors or those who want to take a more active role in running the magazine. We work with writers from different backgrounds and skillsets and want to share our platform with people who might otherwise be intimidated to write a story, edit a sound piece, or make a film. We are also going to be releasing a more dynamic platform to accompany the main magazine and the more in-depth pieces we offer on the site.

From Diyala to Dearborn, the stories of Iraq are endless.

"Strength in the Face of Fighter Jets," by Nidal El Khairy (2013), originally published on shakomako.net and republished with permission.

18| The Save the Tigris and Marshes Campaign: An Interview with Nadia al-Baghdadi
22 September 2014

Launched in March 2012, the Save the Tigris and Marshes Campaign appeared in reaction to plans by the Turkish government to construct the Ilısu Dam, which drew controversy first because, once complete, it would flood the ancient Kurdish city of Hasankeyf in Turkey, and second because it would have a major, perhaps devastating environmental impact downstream in Iraq and beyond. The campaign is closely associated with both the Iraqi Civil Society Solidarity Initiative—a network of Iraqi civil society organizations and international groups—and the Iraq Social Forum, first held in September 2013.[51] What follows is an interview with the campaign's Baghdad coordinator, Nadia al-Baghdadi, who discusses how the campaign developed, how she got involved, and broader issues of organizing in Iraq during the recent years of war, occupation, and hope.

Ali Issa (AI): What is the Save the Tigris and Marshes Campaign and how did you get involved in it?

Nadia al-Baghdadi (NB): Well, it is a regional and international campaign, launched to protect the Tigris River from Turkish dams, specifically the Ilısu Dam. This is not really a new issue though. Years before the 2003 occupation, the Iraqi people were cut off from the outside world. The sanctions were not just economic. A sanctions-like environment preceded the formal economic ones by decades. That is to say that we were unaware when there were plans to put dams up on the Tigris River right outside of Iraq's borders. We simply did not know about them. One day in 2012, when I saw a petition on Facebook, I was surprised and wondered why they were collecting signatures.

I read the petition and learned that there were massive projects underway on the Tigris that were threatening it. This was a moment when we were going through a serious drought in the area—very little rainfall—that was exacerbated by the reduced amount of water coming from the river. This was also an untouched issue because decades had passed since any supposed government plans were disrupted by wars the Iraqi government fought, which in general pushed successive Iraqi regimes to ignore the issue. To be honest, at the time I had no idea how a grassroots campaign operated: the steps and what must be done. I started posting hysterically on Facebook and telling all my friends about the dam, that this was something very serious. I really was afraid. I was terrified because it really is terrifying. Here we had a gigantic dam, about sixty-five kilometers from the Iraqi border, and now the Turkish government has begun the second stage of building another dam—and that dam is hydroelectric. This second dam is forty-five kilometers from the Ilısu Dam—from which it will receive its water—which will reduce Iraq's water to half its current levels. Even these present levels are creating serious issues in central and southern Iraq. Tribes have begun battling over potable water. Many large areas of farmland have already dried up. The filling of the Ilısu reservoirs has not even begun yet, but due to the drought and consecutive dry seasons, we are having these problems. What is going to happen here when they start filling those reservoirs? There are of course international conventions that require Turkey to discuss their plans with neighboring countries—with Iraq and Syria—and to make plans for portioning the water. Turkey, though, rejects all of that. This really horrified me. One of my friends had an idea of how we could develop our work and direct our efforts, but he did not have the time. So, he asked me if I would like to contact the campaign directly and offer what we could. I said sure. I have some time, but you have the experience. He said, "Don't worry, I am behind you." He taught me how to look up the campaign organizers' e-mail addresses and ask them what they might need.

AI: All this was the start of 2012?

NB: The campaign began in March 2012, and I first contacted them in July. Soon after that, I started to meet the other organizers on Skype. Little by little I started to take on projects. They said we have leaders in Iraqi Kurdistan but not in Baghdad, so I got more active. We have Mutanabbi Street in Baghdad, which is where artists, thinkers, and activists meet. I went there and did some very simple work: passing around the petition and collecting signatures by hand. Unfortunately, the number of Internet users in Iraq in 2012 was very small. The number is higher now, but people primarily use it for sending e-mails, shopping online, and playing video games. Working on the ground has real benefits. Gathering signatures by itself is not going to get you anywhere, but it is a way to start talking to people, a way to start describing the problem. Media personnel also frequent Muttanabi Street to cover what people are doing there. We also went to other areas of Baghdad, including Zawraa Park and Karrada. Little by little, I had about twenty-five youths collecting signatures in Zawraa Park. There they met up with a team of journalists from Basra, so they talked and built a connection. Our work on Facebook also took us further out to Amman, Jordan, the United Arab Emirates, and even New Zealand. Momentum started to build. I am still in contact with our partners in Turkey, Iran, Kurdistan, and Italy. More recently, some activists from the United States and United Kingdom joined us.

There were several sites for the campaign: Turkey itself, Sulaymaniyah, and Basra where we held a conference. Even in Amman we held a session. By the time we held our most recent conference in early 2014, the Ministry of Environment attended. This was after months of trying to get in contact with the ministry. Sadly, official channels in Iraq are extremely complex and difficult to reach. The channels that you want to use to talk to an official require a "contact." An informal contact may be a relative, for example, or someone who works for and is protected by a particular minister or official, and who might get you in so you can request a meeting. This is something the entire society goes through: if you contact anyone by e-mail, or any other way, you just cannot expect an answer.

AI: Did you ever get a direct response from Iraqi officials?

NB: By 22 March 2014, we were able to bring together several ministries and the local Baghdad government, and sat them down at one table. We described the situation, told them we have demands, and laid out our whole platform. The minister of environment gave us his description of the dangers that the Ilısu Dam poses to Iraq, and the minister of agriculture gave his ministry's opinion, and so on. The minister of water said they had prepared plans. We said that we have particular recommendations: (1) we must pressure Turkey, (2) we must collaborate internationally, (3) we must publish peer-reviewed studies, and (4) we must try to raise a legal case against Turkey for not sharing its plans with Iraq and obeying international conventions. But I am certain that they received our recommendations and stuck them in a bottom drawer somewhere. In the end, that is what happened.

After that, there was a flood season with heavy rains in Baghdad and elsewhere. Then there were religious holidays, a terrorist attack, and many bloody days, until the Islamic State took Mosul in June and life stopped all over Iraq. Politics stopped completely. In March we had the conference, in April there were the elections, and it was not until August that they put together a government. That is where we are today.

Unfortunately, there are no functioning institutions in Iraq. Political process comes down to the whims and political desires of individuals. If you are working with some official, and their time is up, his replacement has no relationship to the work the first person was doing. There is no continuity. You have to start with him from scratch. No institutions, just individuals.

AI: What are the methods of pressure you have at your disposal to use against decision-makers? What kind of reach and impact did your tactics have and how did they help your outreach?

NB: What we have now is press releases. Whenever a Turkish official or minister visited Iraq we sent out a release that said, "Take advantage of this visit to open negotiations." This has been a key tool in getting our message out to as many people as possible. As far as reach, we say truthfully that this dam will affect each and every region of Iraq. The Tigris flows from the north to south. The Kurds will also be affected by the shortage of water, though they rely mostly on rainwater. But the area in Turkey where they are building the dam is Kurdish and contains artifacts that are four millennia old, perhaps older. These will be destroyed. So, a part of Kurdish cultural heritage is also under direct threat. Of course the Euphrates runs through the western regions of Iraq. But the Euphrates is dead. At this point, its water is not drinkable. People cannot use it. Many animals and plants are also not able to survive off of it. If not for the Tigris and the transfer of water that is happening, those areas would be completely dry.

Anbar has had a particular security and political situation for far longer than when the media started to cover the topic in 2013. Despite that, there were activists in Anbar who got in contact with our campaign, and said they would welcome and fund a visit to their region, and they invited us to hold a conference there. In the period of three days, we visited Amman, Basra, and Dhi Qar, giving workshops and the like. After that, we were supposed to visit Anbar and other central areas, but things got worse with al-Qaʿida, so we could not complete our journey.

AI: What is your explanation for the success of this cross-movement, cross-sectarian campaign? How does it relate to the sectarianism that dominates images of Iraq?

NB: I would not say the view that the world has of Iraq is completely incorrect, but it is seriously lacking. Our civil society is taking baby steps, but it is stumbling. The pressures are great, but the insistence and perseverance is greater. At the 2013 Iraq Social Forum, we saw that, despite the wars and the economic and cultural sanctions, we have youth who are energized to act and have very clear visions and specific goals. These are qualities that, unfortunately, our generation of Iraqis does not have. Sadly, the past has ruined and twisted us. We are sick, psychologically. What we have seen has made us sick. It is not small what we have gone through. It means that we have gone through a split. These youth are different, they wanted to change things and they worked together. In the end, I had reached a point of despair after talking with politicians and doing the media work. Even the media is tied to parties and agendas. They would not publish what we wanted. If an official stood with us, then the story would become all about his presence, about this politician being there for the Tigris. But the youth did not care about those politics, so I saw another face of civil society work, wherein the government produces the barriers. It produces many, many barriers.

AI: What is the source of these obstacles?

NB: Some of the social justice campaigns have reached a critical mass, but [they] always come up against the "wall of the sectarian quota system [*muhasasa*]." This system leaves no room for integrity.

The approval for our space was met with rejection from someone within the *same city agency* that initially approved it . . . the rejection came from one political bloc while the approval came from another. This sectarian system has destroyed the country. We get to the point of having an issue gain international recognition and symbolic support, but come up against this wall. This same system creates a deep lack of competence in Iraqi officials. This is why obstacles to organizing persist in Iraq.

AI: What role do international forces play in these dynamics? How about the present rise of IS?

NB: Two comments are enough here. When the US occupation started, it dismantled the army, the police, and the Ministry of Culture. It left the country without those institutions. Just imagine. The lack of security and the amount of unemployment have left people feeling oppressed and defeated, with every kind of negative feeling that people could have about themselves.

My brother was one of those taken in by the US occupation. They took him around 2008, and they interrogated him for an entire week, repeating one question over and over: Are you Sunni or Shiʿa? I do not come from a religious family. So Sunni, Shiʿi, these categories are not even in our systems. For a week they kept asking him, "What are you?" And he would say, "I am Iraqi. That is all I am. None of your business." My ex-husband, who is from Falluja, was also put in US jails, and he came out completely brainwashed. In the past, he would go out, have a drink, but since his detention, he became much more religious. With hundreds of thousands of people being rounded up, locked up for a few months with access to sectarian books only, they were inevitably impacted by sectarian ideology. Combine this with a bad government full of failed policies, and you have a disastrous situation. Indeed, the Shi'i government and its sectarian treatment of Sunnis could not have been worse. After 2004, there were identity killings. These are the kinds of things created by the sectarian divisions. Instead of tolerance and coexistence, we became closed societies that fear the other. All this easily leads to something like IS. Sectarianism was forced on us, planted among us by outside forces. Of course Iraqi forces helped, but the main engines were external, using Iraqi hands. These are the reasons for the existence of IS.

The effect of the Islamic State is catastrophic in terms of the numbers of lives lost. That refugees were forced out of their homes, and had to witness so much violence and death as they escaped, is a big psychological blow. Then there was the feeling of insecurity when you do get to that safe place. People did try to help: yesterday, for example, here in Baghdad there was a fundraiser where we raised six thousand dollars for internally displaced persons. On the other hand, there is a human dimension. People from Mosul who went down south to Karabala were treated like they were from there. This is something big, that Yazidis—who some people call "devil worshipers"—find Muslims trying to do all they can to help them. So the effect of the Islamic State is devastating, but there is also a way that it is uniting us.

"Harbiyya" (2012) by Ali Eyal

19| The Organization of Women's Freedom in Iraq Now: Interview with Jannat Alghezzi, OWFI's Media Director
28 September 2014

The Organization of Women's Freedom in Iraq (OWFI) was founded in 2004 and is prominent for its work on gender justice in Iraq and its cross-movement approach. Among two of OWFI's recent, ongoing projects are producing the women's rights-focused Al Mousawat *newspaper—and web newsletter—for the past seven years and leading a campaign against those responsible for the horrific damage done to the small northern Iraqi town of Hawija by a US military installation.⁵² More recently, OWFI has taken on part of the work in providing shelter and safety for women escaping mass rape and ethnic cleansing by IS while simultaneously opposing US airstrikes and intervention.⁵³ In the interview below, OWFI's media director Jannat Alghezzi discusses all this and more.*

Ali Issa (AI): How would you describe the evolution of civil society work in Iraq?

Jannat Alghezzi (JA): I started working with Iraqi civil society in 2008. At that time, this was a new experiment in Iraq. Right now we cannot say that it is as new. At this point, we have been working for almost a decade in civil society organizations here in Baghdad. In 2008, when these organizations started, the situation was different: about three thousand organizations were registered in Baghdad alone. Now, if you asked how many are really working in the greater Baghdad area, the answer would be about ten. In my view, the organizations that are working are the sole ray of light that remains in Iraq. The violence here goes on and on. There is a sector of society that is deeply impacted by this, especially liberatory feminist women. Why do I feel that the United States played such a decisive role in this? Because when they came in 2003, they were the main engines of empowerment for the Islamic political parties that rule now.

AI: How did you start working with OWFI? Had you worked with other groups before?

JA: Before working with OWFI, I worked with several organizations in central Iraq and in the south with a group called Human Rights Monitor Association, and after that, I worked with another called International Research and Exchange (IREX). I also worked specifically on a program called Building Bridges Through Technology (BBTT). But with those groups, my connection to them focused on technology, on the practical level. It did not touch the lives of others. What pushed me to go deeper into OWFI was its ability to confront what we always call "our traditions," which punish women with honor killings and other practices. OWFI was the only group that would face these old, tired practices in our society. So this was what mainly tied me to the group and what drove me to step up and ask to volunteer with them.

AI: How has your work with them evolved?

JA: Over the years my role in OWFI has definitely changed. In the beginning all I did was office and administrative work. Now I am part of the leadership. We make the decisions about the direction that OWFI will take. I am currently working on three main projects: (1) the Women's Empowerment Project, which includes protecting women from honor killings, and I am responsible for a safe house for women and girls; (2) the "Equality Radio" [*Al Mousawat*] station, which is the voice of OWFI and for which I am the executive director; and (3) our recent LGBT project, which focuses on queer people. Back in 2008, I did not even know what "queer" meant. Things have really changed.

AI: What exactly is the Women's Empowerment Project?

JA: Well, I first got to know OWFI as a victim of this society. I had some problems with my family, and they threatened me. "If you do not straighten up, we are going to kill you." So OWFI really helped me with its shelter program. In 2007, I spent time in one of OWFI's safe houses. It saved my life. Right now I could be a number at a morgue with my name on a stone. That program also helped me see that I was not to blame for the situation I was in. You know what it means for someone to get a second chance? This was my second chance, so when I got back into society I wanted to work on these issues. I understood so clearly what this movement was and how it could change the lives of women. Society mistreats women based on their gender: just because they are women, they are victims. So, when I started working on this, I went to a lot of trainings to get stronger as an organizer. This is the work that the empowerment project does. Since 2008, our safe houses have increased and developed. Even in the current circumstances, with the presence of IS and various militias, we are able to open new safe houses, like the one we started ten days ago. There is a kind of madness to our work . . . .

AI: How do you see this relating to other issues in society?

JA: As for the connection between gender and economic justice, we always say that the first step for the liberation of women is economic liberation. If women were free economically, they could take control of their situation. What we have now is a society where women always ask their husbands for money or their brothers or sons—the roots of the patriarchal system. So, one of the links between the feminist movement and liberatory feminism is the ability of women to take care of themselves and their families financially.

AI: How broad and deep would you say that OWFI's impact is?

JA: I am not saying that we can change the broader society right now. With the size of the movement in Iraq at present, we are very limited in what we can do and in our reach. What we are doing now is supposed to be the government's responsibility. I mean a government that would support you so you can change laws and more. As it is, we are always confronted by the government and the tribal structure—the system here as a whole. Our movement is small, and our influence—I cannot say that it is large. But at the same time, the impact we do make is like a ray of light. We like to be the place that can ignite a mass movement. I know that I am not going to benefit from the things that I am currently fighting for. My daughter, or perhaps my granddaughter, might gain from what I am doing today. Despite everything, we are optimistic.

AI: What other kinds of political work have OWFI members been a part of?

JA: The main reason OWFI was founded was to build a mass movement that would support women. It is an organization committed to struggle. The year 2011 was very important to us, especially the protests that were happening in Baghdad's Tahrir Square. That kind of action is at the heart of our work. We were one of the movements at that time calling for change. The often-heard demand for "democracy" from those days is because there was nothing of the kind. We were beaten and insulted. I myself was one of the people who were beat down very harshly in Tahrir Square. We were attacked more than once as an organization. The government would not renew our license as a non-governmental organization. So it was, and remains, a fake democracy.

Later in 2013, the Anbar protests were a kind of second wave of the protest movement. We had members who participated from our network—our OWFI branch in Samarra, among others. We also have a partnership with the Federation of Workers' Councils and Unions in Iraq, which was connected to this second wave. So, at that time there was a convergence of many forces. We got up on the podium and spoke, because then the protests involved the tribal leaders and there was a general atmosphere of uprising. But when the vision became centered on injustices toward the Ba'th Party, the focus shifted from our vision for Iraq. We withdrew. At the start, we wanted to be present in a very big way, and our group was very much respected. We sent representatives to meetings, but then things started to take a Ba'thist and fundamentalist bent, which was not the direction we wanted to take.

AI: Many Iraqis I have interviewed noted the way that Nouri al-Maliki repressed these mass demonstrations. What would you say drives this repression?

JA: The problem is not the repression of Maliki or any other figure. It is not about individuals but rather about an entire regime. Our system here is based on sectarianism, on drilling sectarianism deeper and deeper into our society. So you mentioned Maliki, who has been forced out of power, but the system still stands. Nothing has changed. We still face the same issues. For example, Maliki is gone, but our radio station was shut down because we launched a media campaign to criticize the Jaafari Law, a personal status law that the Iraqi Council of Ministers introduced in March 2014. According to Human Rights Watch, the law would "restrict women's rights in matters of inheritance and other rights after divorce, make it easier for men to take multiple wives, and allow girls to be married from the age of nine."[54] Because of our criticism, the radio has been shut down for about two months, even with our "new" government. The police and Interior Ministry security forces came, as well as people from the media and communications authority, and they shut the station down. It is an entire regime of Islamists and tribal leaders allied with them that rule. So, that oppression is coming from the tribal heads that are now in the government and from the systems that are built on those tribal bases to begin with. It is not a matter of the individuals involved.

AI: What is the role of Iraq's present constitution?

JA: Well, historically, Iraq has always faced some form of these problems. But I think in the recent period, the holes in the constitution are especially glaring. These elements of the constitution have divided society. What the Bremer plan brought to Iraq, the sectarian quota system, was not built on competence, but on sectarian quotas. World governments, led by the United States, established and backed this idea. The present moment demonstrates this failure. Government militias control half of Iraq, and men with a hyper-reactionary religious vision control the other half. That leaves us, the secular ones, the civil society organizers, trapped between these two sides.

AI: What role do other regional and international forces play?

JA: As I said, several countries have intervened in Iraqi affairs. Iran represents for us the Shiʻi wing, and Saudi Arabia and Turkey represent the Sunni wing. It is about the leaders of states with religious capital preserving their own power and interests. Turkey considers Mosul to still be a state in its Ottoman Empire, and Iran is very invested in projecting influence over Shiʻa communities. Every country has its particular interests and its point people who are supporting these interests from within Iraq. For us, inside OWFI, we do not take sides—that this country did wrong and that one did wrong. It is a regional question, one of oil and borders, which is a context larger than a small group like ours can intervene in.

AI: What do you think the future holds?

JA: At the present, the future is looking bleak. This entire regime is like a house built on a shoddy foundation. You cannot expect a structure like that to stand. Without a secular, equality-based constitution, nothing will improve. This is my personal opinion and not that of OWFI. At the present moment, there is a war from both sides against secularism and civil society. Very recently some of the organizations here in Baghdad have lost their way because of their loyalty to the Iraqi army. Leaders of organizations went out with the army, the "popular mobilization," and Shiʻi militias against IS. But beyond being against IS, they lost their distanced perspective. Civil organizations working on people's issues should not go out and take those positions. So many of the organizations lost their way due to their backing of political parties in power. When a party backs a group, the group is then forced to stand and appear as a part of that political formation. So, I do not know; if you are asking me about the future, right now the future is looking bleak.

AI: How important is international movement support to OWFI?

JA: We have support coming from many parts of the world, and this gives us strength—that there is an international movement that can stand with us. If it were not for that global support, we would have been "liquidated" here in Baghdad, as they say. But because we know there are supporters of what we are doing in Baghdad, we take risks and know someone is going to be asking about us.

We know there are supporters and people who understand what we are doing here in Iraq. That a group committed to struggle and gender rights, and takes up the responsibilities of a state, even exists, is huge.

20| The Struggle for Justice in Iraqi Kurdistan: An Interview with Akram Nadir
December 2014

Akram Nadir is the international representative of the Federation of Workers' Councils and Union in Iraq (FWCUI), the Kurdistan Construction Workers' Organization (KCWO), and the Kurdistan Refugee Workers' Association. He was also the co-founder of the Unemployed Workers' Union in Kurdistan back in 1992. Following decades, if not centuries, of repression by successive Baghdad-based regimes—one of the most brutal being Saddam Hussein's—and the 1991 US-led Gulf War in Iraq, the Kurdish Democratic Party (KDP) and the Patriotic Union of Kurdistan (PUK) established the semi-autonomous Kurdistan Regional Government, over which the United States established a no-fly zone from 1991 until 2003. The leaders of the KDP and the PUK are the established "rulers" to which Nadir repeatedly refers. The Islamic State, after June 2014 when it overtook Mosul, has repeatedly attacked Kurdish forces with the US military stepping in and offering assistance.

Ali Issa (AI): How would you describe the general state of politics and organizing in Iraqi Kurdistan today?

Akram Nadir (AN): The mood in Iraqi Kurdistan right now is one of caution and fear. There has been a sharp drop in market activity as well as a long-term suspension of government projects. Unemployment is also up, while migration to Kurdistan's cities keeps growing, since many consider them safer than other Iraqi cities. Thousands of Syrian refugees have also arrived, preceded by refugees from Turkey and Iran.

At the same time, there is now a precious opportunity for political formations—from the nationalist and the religious to the secular and beyond—to create a true alternative platform to the powers that have ruled since 1991. These are the parties that have monopolized power in "democratic" Iraqi Kurdistan, along with the "opposition," which allied with them either behind the scenes or sometimes right out in the open.

AI: Are there forces on the ground in Kurdistan that oppose both the Kurdistan Regional Government and IS?

AN: There are certainly many here who oppose IS as well as the central government in Baghdad, the Kurdish regional government, and US policies, especially US foreign policy. However, the numerous past crises, such as the severe repression based on religious or ethnic identity, have allowed the nationalist parties to convince the people that US intervention is the best assurance that will keep Kurdistan safe from any regional interventions, whether from Iraq's central government, Turkey, Syria, or Iran. Now there are IS attacks on Kurdistan.

Despite these difficulties, over the past few years, people have begun to build awareness of the aims of the 2003 US intervention, which were to secure its economic interests and the interests of the political parties that are its agents.

The opposition I mentioned above has not organized itself to a degree that we can rely on it as an independent force that is given consideration in political equations. Once it reaches that point, it will be a source of social pressure that would further all our work for change. At the same time, the ruling parties have attempted to repress any opposition or union or civil organizing if it does not enjoy their total allegiance or if it opposes their policies here.

AI: What is the state of particular movement struggles in Kurdistan now?

AN: As I alluded to earlier, the conditions with regard to workers, women, and civil society have been deteriorating in Kurdistan, giving the state the chance to militarize and persuade people that these parties' militias should be considered *the* force of security along the region's borders. The government also argues that these militias can "reclaim" areas that are in dispute with the central Iraqi government, such as parts of Kirkuk. These same parties try to posit the present moment as a golden opportunity to achieve independence and embrace a chauvinist nationalism with the backing of regional governments. They also try to deepen the various fissures, sectarian and otherwise, to further their interests and policies, which are built on empty promises. These efforts aim to realize the dream of a Kurdish state and to distract from society's class and humanistic ambitions in order to push for a reactionary and exclusionary politics. This is destined only to divide society further.

The state of working people, especially since IS attacked Mosul, has been fragile: over one hundred and thirty thousand workers have been laid off in the private sector alone. In the public sector, where workers' salaries are tied to the central government, workers in all regions of Kurdistan Iraq have only received eighteen percent of what they are owed. This disparity was actually there before the emergence of IS and, now, has merely intensified.

Despite all of those obstacles, political parties, workers' organizations, feminist and leftist groups are mounting a challenge to the fascism that emerges from the government's policies. Two such groups are the Organization of Women's Freedom in Iraq and unions affiliated with the Federation of Workers' Councils and Unions in Iraq. The Kurdistan Refugee Workers' Association is of course also rising in importance due to the current moment we are experiencing. Real alternatives are not going to come from those in power or from a formal opposition, especially now after their "reconciliation" under the banner of fighting IS. In reality, all of these parties took part in diminishing the spirit of revolt and silencing demands for fundamental change that the people of Kurdistan, especially the youth, were putting out in February 2011. In sit-ins inspired by the revolts of Tunisia and Egypt, which lasted for weeks in and around Sulaymaniyah at Azadi Square, people called for "the regime to fall." Over the course of those months, dozens of youth were killed or injured and hundreds imprisoned. Despite that, ongoing repression and all the events since have not extinguished the movement. I still believe it is what we need now.

Conclusion

To be truly radical is to make hope possible rather than despair convincing.
Raymond Williams, *Resources of Hope*[55]

What the interviews and reports in *Against All Odds* clearly demonstrate is that over the last ten years, a wide cross section of people from Iraq have boldly waged popular struggle: from blocking oil privatization in 2007 and mobilizing for the mass protests of 2011 to the present moment where shelters for women escaping IS double as political education and organizing training spaces. Visionary Iraqis are dreaming and acting.

From these particular campaigns I would like to draw four general points. One, the near-total lack of media coverage of these struggles is itself part of the dehumanizing violence Iraqis face every day. Two, these popular movements do not come out of a vacuum. They are intimately connected to an Iraqi history of organizing, vision, and tenacity as well as regional and global events, from the 2011 Egyptian uprising to Occupy Wall Street. Three, to be relevant, efforts to act in solidarity with Iraqis must be keyed to local demands—Iraqi demands *for* something—emerging on the ground, and spoken in their own words. Finally, that Iraq is neither exceptional in being treated as a hopeless place, nor is the United States the sole force behind its grave challenges: other regional and global players are also implicated in its many crises. These four points must be taken into account if the dominant conceptual landscape on Iraq is to be challenged and replaced, at all levels: from popular culture to policy briefs.

It should go without saying that events like the fifty-three-day-long leather worker strike, which took place in 2010—described in appendix I below—did not emerge from a void. "The vitality of [Iraq's] history" that Vijay Prashad writes about in the foreword, is something Iraqi organizers often refer to and are directly propelled by. Beyond allusions to the 1920 resistance to British occupation, there has been a lineage of grassroots organizing and a complex identification with Iraqi identities that makes progressive organizing in Iraq possible now. An understanding of the political legacies of Iraq's leftist movements[56] is required to explain how the present-day movements in Iraq continue to fight, win supporters, and achieve gains, amid a multi-pronged and sustained attack on the hopes and dreams they are fighting for.

How do those hopes relate to the violent and profoundly unequal material conditions that make up the recent history of Iraq? How should that reality be portrayed? No one can deny the importance of documenting the horrors of mass murders by foreign occupation as well as local forces, growing sectarian violence, and a litany of other shocking experiences that Iraqis continue to be exposed to. My Iraqi contacts on the ground though, demand that portrayals of existing conditions and dynamics start with *their own words*. The interviews in this book have shown that telling these stories can and should be done through describing the local efforts to resist and replace repressive systems. For example, should we discuss the oppression of Iraqi women? Absolutely, but without disregarding the experiences of activists like Aya Al Lamie, Jannat Alghezzi, and Yanar Mohammed who protested, organized, and were repressed precisely for exhibiting their power and potential to challenge patriarchy within and without Iraqi society. The same approach can and should be taken for many of Iraq's daunting challenges across social spheres, from economic and environmental to sectarian and so on.

Further opportunities for engagement with various other struggles in Iraq present themselves every day. Attempts by the Iraqi labor movement to pass a labor law that would sanction their activities are ongoing, as are demands for wage increases and improved working conditions. Demonstrations and workplace occupations across industrial sectors in Babel, Baghdad, and Basra in December 2014 up to the moment of this writing underscore that fact.[57]

Documenting and reporting on everyday political and social life in Iraq remains a very dangerous task. Indeed, as the Committee to Protect Journalists has shown, the past three years have been the "most deadly" for journalists in Iraq.[58] Uday al-Zaidi is a living example of this. Shortly after a December 2014 Al Jazeera Arabic appearance, where he voiced outspoken positions against the US and Iranian roles in contemporary Iraqi politics, Zaidi was arrested by Iraqi security forces in Shatrah city in southern Iraq on 9 January 2015.[59] Reportedly having undergone torture, he was released on 21 January 2015, and is now in recovery.

As a preliminary step in remedying the gap in covering conditions on the ground in Iraq, I hope that *Against All Odds* can also speak to other parts of the world that are often solely associated with horror and despair: Afghanistan, Somalia, the Democratic Republic of Congo, Mexico, the list goes on. How have people in those places been building hope and political possibility? To seriously pursue that question is to cast off the label of "destroyed" or "failed" that forecloses any deeper engagement. The people of Mexico face a repressive state, US exploitation, and non-state actors in the form of narco-trafficker kingpins. While the contexts of these struggles differ from those in Iraq, they nonetheless have much in common, as would the strategies needed to drop the "hopeless" label they share. Dialoguing across borders about how people are resisting such powerful forces would illuminate broader global patterns of repression and resistance as well as allow for building solidarity around the world.

A global focus on the US role, especially from within the US Left, has obscured other dynamics at play in Iraq and elsewhere. As we have seen, Iraqis are deeply aware of the destructive nature of US foreign policy and actions in Iraq's history and present. In addition, however, Iraqis face challenges from regional actors, as well as entrenched local dynamics such as the shaming of female rape survivors by heads of households, and their ostracization from family, neighborhood, and/or tribe, for example.

Shedding light on the US role alone—crucial as it may be—at the expense of other central dynamics that have and continue to shape everyday realities in Iraq, does a disservice to Iraqis who have lost life and limb, and continue to make great sacrifices to overcome the many obstacles they face. In other words, the harmful US-centrism that has marked analysis of, and action concerning, what is happening in Iraq not only emerges from successive US administrations but also in the assumptions of its critics and opposition. This creates a profound disconnect between Iraqis on the ground and the rest of the world.

To sum up, let us take the concrete case of the Organization of Women's Freedom in Iraq. This group—which provides shelters and politicizes members like Jannat Alghezzi, who fled threats made by her own family members—is mounting sustained resistance to the Iraqi government-proposed Jaafari Personal Status Law, a law that severely restricts women's choice in marriage matters. This resistance, meanwhile, is informed by a deep awareness of US, Iranian, and regional attempts to dominate Iraqi politics. Imagining accountability to those particular political commitments gives us a deep lesson for what solidarity with Iraqis must look like today, and reveals the limitations of a pure focus on either US empire, growing Iranian influence, or the threat and violence of IS. Clearly, Iraqis on the ground are profoundly affected by and are responding to all these forces.

Conclusion

Concrete stories of trying to pass a labor law or maintain Iraqi control of its oil and gas resources compel us to imagine what kind of world Iraqis *do* want, and how activists the world over and thinkers might stand with those efforts. We might also learn how these visions—against all odds—can inspire our own, wherever and whenever we are.

Ali Issa
Brooklyn, New York
March 2015

Appendix I

Victory for Leather Industry Workers as Strikes Spread[60]
2 January 2010

After a fifty-three-day strike—the longest in Iraq since 1931—won workers in the leather industry the release of long promised safety benefits and back wages, FWCUI-affiliated unions are at it again, this time organizing Baghdad cotton factory workers and announcing a strike for similar demands, now entering its nineteenth day. There is yet another strike, this one in the industrial area of Nahrawan (east of Baghdad) at al-Thalal brick factory. This strike began on 23 December. If these actions are any indication, organizing in the industrial sector is really catching fire in Iraq. In the face of such effective and uncompromising direct action, the Iraqi authorities—surprise, surprise—have stepped up their attempts to interfere by "relocating" organizers to remote offices or simply firing them. The most threatening of these attempts, though, takes the form of planned union federation elections, which the FWCUI considers to be a sham meant only to confer legitimacy on the state-backed federation. This then may lead to the very Ba'thist move of banning all "unrecognized" unions.

Statement on the Victory of the Leather Industry Workers

> After one of the longest strikes in the history of the Iraqi workers' movement, the workers in leather production achieved a historic victory, when the administration agreed to pay safety benefits. The strength and endurance of the strike, which lasted over fifty days, was in the unity and determination of the workers, and their singular focus on their demands and organizing. The organizers showed an ability to lead the strike and maintain the determination among the ranks of the workers for more than seven weeks. The lack of response among the organizers and the rank-and-file to the promises made by the administration, and their insistence on making their demands a reality, was a result of valuable experience gained by the workers over the course of long

negotiations. That meant hearing the promises and foot-dragging by the administration, which would often conclude with non-binding talk about the future. This was a triumph and an eloquent lesson for us workers, which we will be sure to learn from. That lesson is not to respond to any kind of promises, which intend to slow or extinguish the movement of workers. The victory of the workers in the leather industries is the beginning of a new drive for the workers movement in the public sector and all sectors. The workers in the Ministry of Industry organized several demonstrations, marches, and gatherings to call for what they were owed, the last of which was the heroic demonstration that faced the Iraqi security forces, who opened fire on the cornered protesters on 6 October 2009. Thereafter, the state did not offer anything but broken promises. Let the victory of the workers in the leather industry push for the building of a broad-based movement toward realizing the workers' demands in the entire Ministry of Industry for back pay and safety benefits. Now the workers in the leather industry have just achieved another important goal as part of a heroic movement, which is organizing their labor unions and groups autonomously without the interference of the administration or state officials. Let us work for the freedom to organize and repeal the laws of Saddam Hussein's regime that does not allow for the right to organize in the public sector. Long live the workers' demands for safety benefits! Long live the workers' demands for the right to organize!

The Federation of Workers' Councils and Unions in Iraq
7 December 2009

Appendix II

Contacts published on 8 December 2011, by the Popular Movement to Save Iraq, in their statement "Friday of Occupation's Defeat."

1. Baghdad: Thurgham al-Zaidi, Sana al-Dalaymi, Uday al-Zaidi
2. Mosul: Ghanim al-Abad, Khalid Juma
3. Basra: Mr. Awath al-Abdan, Kamil Ahmad al-Ghathban
4. Salah al-Din: Khalaf Jasim, Hashim al-Hamdani
5. Najaf: Mr. Abu Ameer al-Arathi, Abu Jasim al-Bayati
6. Anbar: Mr. Rahim al-Mahmadi, Layth al-Dalaymi
7. al-Amara: Mr. Faruq al-Mahmadawi, Abu al-Hasan al-Akili
8. Nasariyah: Saud al-Khafaji, Abu Tayba al-Saidi
9. Diyala Province: Mr. Abu Azawi
10. Kirkuk: Mr. Harby al-Amash

Appendix III

Organizations and Initiatives featured in *Against All Odds: Voices of Popular Struggle in Iraq* (with website or Facebook page if available):

Electricity Utility Workers Union

Federation of Workers' Councils and Unions in Iraq, http://on.fb.me/1xe5yDP

General Federation of Iraqi Workers in Basra, http://bit.ly/1FIBwT9

The Great Iraqi Revolution, http://on.fb.me/19wVQYA

Iraqi Civil Society Solidarity Initiative, http://bit.ly/1w97eyo

Iraqi Federation of Oil Unions

Kurdistan Construction Workers' Organization

Kurdistan Refugee Workers' Association

The Popular Movement to Save Iraq, http://on.fb.me/1CerDbS

Organization of Women's Freedom in Iraq, http://bit.ly/1DY2fth

Sada, which was a transnational project that supported emerging artists in Iraq, closed in April 2015, http://bit.ly/1ANuhX7

Save the Tigris and Marshes Campaign, http://bit.ly/1BaXUzn

shakomako.net

Solidarity and Brotherhood Yazidi Organization

Notes

1 Sinan Antoon, "Wrinkles on the Wind's Forehead," *Banipal Magazine of Modern Arab Literature* 18, Autumn 2003, accessed January 12, 2015, http://bit.ly/1yWOkfk.

2 Nadje Al-Ali and Deborah Al-Najjar, *We are Iraqis: Aesthetics and Politics in a Time of War* (Syracuse: Syracuse University Press, 2013), xxvi.

3 Patrick Cockburn, "Diary," *London Review of Books* 28, no. 7 (2006), 34-5, accessed January 7, 2015, http://bit.ly/1xTi8MB.

4 Patrick Cockburn, "Is it the End of Sykes-Picot? Patrick Cockburn on the War in Syria and the Threat to the Middle East," London Review of Books 35, no. 11 (2013), 3-5, accessed January 7, 2015, http://bit.ly/1hUfxxP.

5 Sabr Darwish, "Zahran Alloush Eastern Ghouta's 'King of Kings': From the Regime's Prisons to its Warm Bosom," [In Arabic], *Al Hayat*, January 14, 2015, accessed January 18, 2015 http://bit.ly/1Al1erA.

6 Ali Issa, Iraq Left: On Iraqi Organizing and Movement Building Now, accessed January 7, 2015, http://bit.ly/1ItkapE.

7 For more on Kurdish civil society organizing see: http://bit.ly/1Ig8TdS

8 Sada, accessed March 24, 2015, http://sadairaq.org/.

9 The Great Iraqi Revolution's Facebook page, "Maliki's Government and the Suppression of Friday Demonstrations," [In Arabic], Facebook video, 3:00, March 18, 2011, accessed January 7, 2015, http://on.fb.me/1Au9uHW.

10 Peter Graff, "Two Die, 14 Wounded in Iraq Prison Riot: Police," Reuters, March 13, 2011, accessed January 7, 2015, http://reut.rs/1xHy9a2.

11 Scott Horton, "A Soaring Prison Population in Iraq," *Harper's Magazine*, August 25, 2007, accessed January 7, 2015, http://bit.ly/1HQz7DK.

12 Inter Press Service, "Anti-government Protests Erupt across Iraq," *The Electronic Intifada*, March 7, 2011, accessed January 7, 2015, http://bit.ly/1wlulLb.

[13] Support the Iraqi Youth Uprising in Tahrir Square, "Communiqué Number 16 on the Day of Salvation Sit-in on April 9th," February 25, 2011, accessed January 7, 2015, http://bit.ly/1AudhF6.

[14] Uday al-Zaidi, "Supplement to the Day of Salvation–Communiqué Number 17 –Locations of the Sit-ins in Baghdad and Iraqi Provinces," March 22, 2011, accessed January 7, 2015, http://bit.ly/1w1x1s1.

[15] Leila Fadel, "U.S. Seeking 58 Bases in Iraq, Shiite Lawmakers Say," *McClatchy DC*, June 9, 2008, accessed January 7, 2015, http://bit.ly/1w1yjDm.

[16] Michael Gisick, "U.S. Base Projects Continue in Iraq Despite Plans to Leave," *Stars and Stripes*, June 1, 2010, accessed January 7, 2015, http://1.usa.gov/1tM1dYy.

[17] Serena Chaudhry, "Iraqi Shoe-Thrower Arrested for Supporting Protesters," Reuters, February 24, 2011, accessed January 7, 2015, http://reut.rs/1y1dbTG.

[18] "Sit-Ins in Front of US Bases in Iraq," [In Arabic], Al Jazeera Arabic, April 3, 2011, accessed January 7, 2015, http://bit.ly/1zVEkDT.

[19] The Great Iraqi Revolution's Facebook page, [In Arabic], accessed January 8, 2015, http://on.fb.me/19wVQYA.

[20] "Iraqi Protesters Throw Their Shoes at American Helicopters," YouTube video, 2:02, posted by "Zerocracy," April 13, 2011, accessed January 13, 2015 http://bit.ly/19wpLRF.

[21] The Great Iraqi Revolution's Facebook page, "One of the Heroes of Ahrar Square," [In Arabic], Facebook video, 3:16, April 24, 2011, accessed January 8, 2015, http://on.fb.me/1yUXyyu.

[22] The Great Iraqi Revolution's Facebook page, "From the Lens of Our Correspondent Imad al-Iraqi-The People Want to Topple the Regime, Ahrar Square," [In Arabic], Facebook video, 0:41, April 23, 2011, accessed January 8, 2015, http://on.fb.me/1IvRfRK.

[23] "Iraq Authorities Must Halt Attacks on Protesters," Amnesty International, April 11, 2011, accessed January 19, 2015, http://bit.ly/1AVNuBB.

[24] Reuters, "Iraqi Oil Workers Protest over Pay, Threaten Strike," *Khaleej Times*, May 9, 2011, accessed January 11, 2015, http://bit.ly/1ORb1gy.

25 Campaña Estatal contra la Ocupación y por la Soberanía de Iraq, [National Campaign against the Occupation and for Iraqi Sovereignty], Iraq Solidaridad, accessed January 11, 2015, http://bit.ly/1AEPEHv.

26 Muhanad Mohammed, "Iraq PM Sets 100 Day Deadline for Government after Protests," Reuters, February 27, 2011, accessed January 11, 2015, http://bit.ly/1ICDPmR.

27 "General Strike in Nineveh to Condemn Repression," [In Arabic], Al Jazeera Arabic, April 26, 2011, accessed January 11, 2015, http://bit.ly/17xdQlz.

28 "Iraq: Protesters Detained, at Risk of Torture," Amnesty International, June 2, 2011, accessed January 11, 2015, http://bit.ly/1ICJ85Y.

29 Ali Issa, "Maliki Runs out of Days," The Indypendent, June 7, 2011, accessed January 11, 2015, http://bit.ly/14IVD3l.

30 "The Kidnapping of the Activist Thurgham al-Zaidi," [In Arabic], Popular Movement to Save Iraq, June 30, 2011, accessed January 11, 2015, http://bit.ly/1BW87yL.

31 Support Iraqi Protestors in the Great Iraqi Revolution Facebook page, "New Statement Concerning Next Friday," [In Arabic], Facebook photograph, July 18, 2011, accessed January 11, 2015, http://on.fb.me/14KAC7K.

32 "Alstom Grid Wins Major Iraq Contract," Iraq Business News, July 5, 2011, accessed January 11, 2015, http://bit.ly/1xdo7It.

33 Al-Bab al-Sharqi Facebook page, [In Arabic], accessed March 26, 2015, http://on.fb.me/1CrRNZI.

34 "Iraqi Leader Backs Syria," Day Press News, August 13, 2011, accessed January 11, 2015, http://bit.ly/1AFktf8.

35 The Great Iraqi Revolution's Facebook page, "Open Letter to the Heroic Syrian Revolution," [In Arabic], Facebook photograph, August 22, 2011, accessed January 11, 2015, http://on.fb.me/1y3i4gu.

36 Yanar Mohammed, "Statement by OWFI President on Kidnapping and Torture of Aya Al Lamie," Jadaliyya, October 1, 2011, accessed January 11, 2015, http://bit.ly/1vDqt3C.

37 Yanar Mohammed, "Message of Solidarity to Occupy Wall Street from the Organization of Women's Freedom in Iraq," *Jadaliyya*, November 1, 2011, accessed April 26, 2015, http://bit.ly/1D3vCXS.

38 Statement from the Preparatory Committee for the Friday of Occupation's Defeat Sit-in, [In Arabic], Al-Rasheed Net, December 8, 2011, accessed January 13, 2015, http://bit.ly/1ADrQHr.

39 Joyce Wagner, "The Shoe Thrower's Brother," Vimeo video, 11:12, June 9, 2011, accessed January 12, 2015, http://bit.ly/1ASaN2R.

40 Serene Assir, "Iraq: The Forgotten Uprising Lives On," Al Akhbar English, February 28, 2012, January 11, 2015, http://bit.ly/1DNhthG.

41 Fuel on the Fire, accessed January 11, 2015, http://bit.ly/1snbIGk.

42 General Federation of Iraqi Workers, "Thugs Attack Workers and Trade Union Offices," July 10, 2012, accessed January 11, 2015, http://bit.ly/1EYfIQ7.

43 Alaa al-Lami, "Iraq: Protestors' Demands Between Rejection and Adoption!" [In Arabic], *Al Akhbar*, January 11, 2013, accessed January 11, 2015, http://bit.ly/1yW7Z4X.

44 For more of Reidar Visser's commentary on mass movements and media coverage in Iraq, see his blog *Iraq and Gulf Analysis*, http://bit.ly/1yW94cT.

45 Wayback Machine Internet Archive, *shakomakoNET*, accessed January 11, 2015, http://bit.ly/17xXzwM.

46 Nadia Daar, "My First Cup of Iraq," *shakomakoNET*, April 9, 2013, accessed January 11, 2015, http://bit.ly/11OfZH1.

47 Mohammed Hazem, "Your Blood or Your Stubbornness," *shakomakoNET*, April 19, 2013, accessed January 11, 2015, http://bit.ly/1raax6Y.

48 "Don't Iraq Iran," RootsAction, accessed January 11, 2015, http://bit.ly/1tYdzSY.

49 To Create an Activist Tool Kit for Iraq: 10 Years Later Facebook page, January 15, 2013, accessed January 11, 2015, http://on.fb.me/1BOqvYj.

50 "Transcript for Jan. 16," *Meet the Press*, NBC News, January 16, 2005, accessed January 11, 2015, http://nbcnews.to/1BRcvRN.

[51] Save the Tigris and Marshes Campaign, Iraqi Civil Society Solidarity Initiative, accessed January 11, 2015, http://bit.ly/1HLVxs0.

[52] "OWFI Report: Hawijah in Crisis and the Legacy of US Bases," *The War Resisters League Blog*, October 5, 2011, accessed January 11, 2015, http://bit.ly/1xdYEOT.

[53] "Suicide, Rape, Murder: Life for Women in Iraq Under ISIS," Huffpost Live video, 6:21, June 24, 2014, accessed January 18, 2015, http://huff.lv/1CITSwi.

[54] "'Al-Masalah' Publishes Text of a Draft of the Jaafari Personal Status Law," Al-Masalah, October 26, 2013, accessed January 11, 2015, http://bit.ly/14JMwiN.

[55] Raymond Williams, *Resources of Hope: Culture, Democracy and Socialism* (New York: Verso, 1989), 209.

[56] Both the Organization of Women's Freedom in Iraq and the Federation of Workers' Councils and Unions in Iraq claim ties to the Worker-Communist Party of Iraq, which was formed in 1993 to oppose both Saddam Hussein's regime as well as US interventions and sanctions.

[57] Al-Washaq Al-Iraqi Facebook Page, "Today in Babel Province Protests to Demand Higher Wages," Facebook video, 0:24, January 26, 2015, accessed February 10, 2015, http://on.fb.me/19wPjxS.

[58] "Most Deadly 3-year Period for Journalists: International Journalists Killed at High Rate in 2014," Committee to Protect Journalists, accessed February 12, 2015, http://bit.ly/1AFDdhY.

[59] Mahmoud Morad, "*In Depth: The Displacement of Sunni Arabs in Iraq*," [In Arabic], Al Jazeera Arabic, YouTube video, 48:17, December 15, 2014, accessed February 12, 2015, http://bit.ly/19GAWaT.

[60] Ali Issa, "Victory for Leather Industry Workers as Strikes Spread," Iraq Left: On Iraqi Organizing and Movement Building Now, January 2, 2010, accessed January 11, 2015, http://bit.ly/19viWQn.

ABOUT TADWEEN PUBLISHING

Tadween Publishing is a publishing house that seeks to institutionalize a new form of knowledge production. A subsidiary of the Arab Studies Institute, Tadween aims both to publish critical texts and to interrogate the existing processes and frameworks through which knowledge is produced, while challenging the barriers, boundaries, and preconceived notions of the mainstream publishing world. Tadween also seeks to elevate the standards of nontraditional media publishing by upholding the peer-review standards applied to traditional scholarship.

For more information about Tadween Publishing and to browse our full catalog of books and pedagogical publications, please visit www.tadweenpublishing.com.

ABOUT WAR RESISTERS LEAGUE

War Resisters League, a national organization with members throughout the United States, has been resisting militarism and war since 1923. Today, as one of the leading radical voices in the antiwar movement, WRL builds solidarity across movements and borders, produces counter-military recruitment materials, creates resources for educators and grassroots organizers, and provides training for nonviolent direct action. WRL organizes campaigns against war and militarism, focusing on connections between and within struggles for peace and liberation. WRL affirms that all war is a crime against humanity and works for the removal of the causes of war, including racism, sexism, and all forms of human exploitation.

Join WRL or find out more about our programs and campaigns at:
warresisters.org
twitter.com/resistwar
facebook.com/resistwar
wrl@warresisters.org

CPSIA information can be obtained at www.ICGtesting.com
Printed in the USA
BVOW11s0337160615

404761BV00003B/3/P

9 781939 067166